# *studies in jazz*

Institute of Jazz Studies, Rutgers University
General Editors: *Dan Morgenstern & Edward Berger*

# THE POLICE CARD DISCORD

Studies in Jazz No. 15

Metuchen, N.J., & London, 1993

The Scarecrow Press and the Institute of Jazz Studies,

# *The Police Card Discord*

## *Maxwell T. Cohen*

Rutgers—The State University of New Jersey

British Library Cataloguing-in-Publication data available

**Library of Congress Cataloging-in-Publication Data**

Cohen, Maxwell T., 1908-
    The police card discord / Maxwell T. Cohen.
    p.    cm.—(Studies in jazz ; no. 15)
    ISBN 0-8108-2638-0 (acid-free paper)
    1. Cohen, Maxwell T., 1908- .   2. Entertainers—
Licenses—New York (N.Y.)   3. Music-halls (Variety the-
aters, cabarets, etc.)—Law and legislation—New York
(N.Y.)   4. Identification cards—Law and legislation—
New York (N.Y.)   5. Police regulations—New York
(N.Y.)
I. Title.   II. Series.
KFX2042.E58C64   1993
323.44′8′0973—dc20                                    93-4173

Then I returned and saw all oppressions that are done under the sun; and behold, the tears of such as were oppressed, and they had no comforter; and on the side of the oppressors there was power. . .

*Ecclesiastes*

Maxwell T. Cohen, the author and the attorney who represented the key players in "The Police Card Cases," J. J. Johnson, Beril ("Bill") Rubenstein, and Johnny Richards (standing from left to right to Cohen's side).

# CONTENTS

# DAN MORGENSTERN
## EDITOR'S FOREWORD

We have become so accustomed to the assertion—by any individual or group—of what is perceived as inalienable rights under whatever constitutional amendment that it must seem quaint to younger readers of this welcome book that there was a time, and not so very long ago, in the city that perhaps rightly considers itself the cultural capital of the world, when a whole group of people, ranging from dishwashers to star performers, could capriciously be deprived of their right to work under the cloak of presumed legality. The only thing these people had in common was that they were in need of employment in establishments where alcoholic beverages were served.

This is the gripping story of one man who took on a veritable cabal from various strata of officialdom, and, by relentless application of logic and decency, succeeded in stripping New York's obscene cabaret card of its guise of legality. Fighting vested political interests, prejudice, apathy and monumental stupidity, Maxwell Cohen represented jazz performers as the vanguard in the fight against a grossly unfair and in essence illegal code, perhaps because jazz performers were its most vulnerable victims.

Max Cohen (whom I have had the pleasure of knowing for many years) is a modest man, and he tells the story of his dedicated battle without blowing his own horn. Yet it is crystal clear that without his patience, professional skill and fearlessness the despised cabaret card would not have been banished until a change in the political climate took place.

At times, there is an Alice in Wonderland quality to the events so soberly reported here, but unfortunately this surrealism is not funny, because what is at stake is not just the right of human beings to earn a livelihood but also, in the case of performing artists, their very right to be what they are. This is what Max Cohen, a quintessentially moral man, understood to be the basic indecency of the cabaret card.

Implacably courteous, never raising his voice, Max Cohen tenaciously stood his ground, not least due to his unshakable conviction that the function of the law is to provide justice. A committed fighter for human and civil rights, Max Cohen has truly been a friend to jazz and to some of the music's greatest practitioners. His battle cry might well have been *Illegitimi non carborandum!* Max Cohen never did let the bastards get him down, and so he won the good fight that he fought so well. This accounting should remind us never to take our rights for granted.

DAN MORGENSTERN
Director
Institute of Jazz Studies
Rutgers—The State
University of New Jersey

# PRELUDE

I knew only one musical genius, an explosive but channelized creative force named Bud Powell. Both artists and critics called him the most creative jazz pianist and composer who ever lived. I was his friend and attorney for several years of his tragic life and career.

The New York Supreme Court file in the County Clerk's Office is three inches thick. The caption on the jacket reads: "In Re [this is written by hand] against [this is printed] Earl Powell [handwritten]—An Alleged Incompetent [rubber-stamped]"; it conveys the essence of the tragic story.

"Re" is the abbreviated form of the Latin "res"—thing or matter—and is also the second note in the natural scale of C Major. "Re" is also the name of the Egyptian sun god, the "Life Force." The word "against" is never used in the proper caption of an incompetency proceeding. It is, however, on this file in boldface type. "An Alleged Incompetent" is rubber-stamped. "Rubber-stamped" is a rich phrase in our language. It means the usual, the commonplace, the same, the ordinary, yet, in this instance, the term was applied to one whose influence on other artists and jazz performers throughout the world was pointedly indicated in the affidavits and exhibits within the file.

Thus, the caption on the file cover is the accurate abbreviated biography of one person; here, the life force in opposition to one Earl "Bud" Powell, musical genius but judicially declared incompetent.

In the file there is a curt order with one of the most amazing provisions ever incorporated in a court-issued document, a judicial mandate without precedent in the history of law or music:

ORDERED, that the incompetent undertake and adhere to a program of medical guidance, assistance and rehabilitation in order to further promote and develop his productivity as a composer and an artist of promise . . .

An exhibit dated August 3, 1954, by Nat Hentoff, stated:

Musicians, I think, are as careful as scientists in assigning any of their living colleagues to the category of "genius" but it is my guess that if any such listing belongs to any musician now alive, it belongs to Bud Powell.

In another affidavit, Hentoff wrote:

With regard to Earl (Bud) Powell, may I point out first that he is internationally respected by musicians and critics as *the most important single influence on the evolution of modern jazz piano*. His development in terms of harmony and rhythmic extensions have contributed to further growth of jazz; and there is not one young pianist here or abroad who has not been markedly influenced by him.

During Bud's mental illness, he performed in public with an upper-space-gazing and distracting grin, given macabre touches by shadowy stage lights. Indeed, he then resembled the skull-like makeup of Lon Chaney in his famous portrayal of the mad musical genius of *The Phantom of the Opera*. The sight of the slight, lonely figure slowly crossing the stage to the piano seemed to inhibit and diminish applause until there was silence when he reached the piano. Bud's stance of loneliness conveyed a subtle overtone—a strange prelude to a remarkable performance of originals and standards.

Performing spontaneously, Bud created counterpoint with ease and dexterity. His inventiveness was so great that the piano became an inadequate and frustrating medium. He would hum raucously, providing yet another counterpoint seeking to extend the scope of the piano. One is reminded of the famous smuggled records of Toscanini's rehearsals with the NBC Symphony Orchestra: there, soaring above the instruments in agonizing frustration, is the Maestro's hoarse singing, adding an extra dimension to an otherwise purely instrumental medium of musical expression.

Bud was about six years old when his father taught him piano. At the age of eight, he began classical training. At about 14, he became interested in jazz, and two years later joined Cootie Williams's band as pianist, composer and arranger.

In 1951, following an arrest on a narcotics charge which was subsequently dismissed, Bud was hospitalized for psychiatric observation and thereafter committed to a state hospital. He was neglected and ignored for months by the hospital authorities. Deterioration and vegetation threatened to become the inevitable termination to what had once been a promising career in music. Fortunately, a sympathetic nurse obtained a hospital piano for Bud and encouraged him to play again.

When Bud Powell was released from the hospital, he was eager to resume his activities as a performer. Music lovers were elated that this great artist would once again appear publicly, and concerned managers wanted to hire him. In order to accept employment in the world-famous jazz club Birdland, Bud was required to obtain from the New York City Police Department a cabaret employee's identification card. Like millions of my fellow New Yorkers, in fact, like millions of music lovers all over the world, I had never heard of this requisite.

Bud applied at the Police Department and his application was rejected. Distressed, he sought my help. On inquiry, I was informed that the application had been denied by the Police Department because of his two convictions. I wrote an appeal to the Deputy Commissioner in charge of the unit which administered the cabaret employee's identification card and explained the circumstances of the arrest and conviction.

The Police Department was informed that the New York State Liquor Authority, which had statutory permission to prohibit the employment of criminals in its discretion, had granted Bud permission to perform in cabarets. Bud's application was again denied by the police.

I had been recommended to Bud as an attorney by Alan Morrison, an editor of *Jet* and *Ebony* magazines. He knew the Deputy Police Commissioner, and together we visited him to plead Bud's case. The Deputy Commissioner granted Bud a temporary card for his Birdland bookings. We were grateful for this, but what of the future? Was Bud to be barred from future employment in the restaurants, cabarets, or clubs selling liquor in New York City by the Police Department, notwithstanding permission from the State Liquor Authority, a superior authority in that area? I discussed the problem with Morrison and with Oscar Goodstein, who had left law practice to become manager of Birdland.

This was the first time that I learned of a monstrous abuse which had deprived over 12,000 otherwise qualified employees of employment as musicians and entertainers in cabarets because of past offenses, notwithstanding evidence of current rehabilitation, marriage, family, and reputation. Untold thousands of porters, dishwashers, cooks, waiters, bartenders, musicians, performers, and other cabaret and restaurant employees may never have applied for cabaret employee identification cards, in anticipation of denial for past offenses and arrests. Thousands of reputable employees had to submit to fingerprinting and pictures for police records. Employers' investments had been wiped out when their licenses were suspended by the Police Department for employing people without cabaret employee identification cards, or for not listing the employee's names and identification card numbers in a record book required to be kept by the employer for that purpose.

The applicant for the identification card was charged a fee by the Police Department. The fee was placed in the Police Pension Fund—a pension exclusively for the police.

The consequences of failure to obtain a cabaret employee identification card were tragic; families were disrupted, individuals uprooted and displaced, rehabilitated offenders discouraged. There was economic and human waste. Crime was not diminished, but laws, constitutional decisions and progressive state social policy were being flouted by the Police Department.

In addition to unknown, unskilled, illiterate or semiliterate applicants or workers, some of the nation's most skilled and talented performers and musicians, welcome everywhere else in the world, many of them representing the U.S. Department of State in troubled areas as part of international cultural exchange programs, had been denied, because of a past criminal offense, sometimes dating back as long as 19 years, the right to work in New York City's liquor-dispensing restaurants and cabarets by the Police Department—truly an instance of "art made tongue-tied by authority, folly, doctor-like, controlling skill . . ."*

I investigated. The "Police Card" system and procedures had never been enacted by the New York City or New York State Legislatures. The Police Department had arrogated to itself the authority to require the possession of identification cards as a requisite for employment, to impose a fee for the card, and to place the money so collected into a Police Pension Fund.

I estimated that over $500,000 had been collected. "It's over one million dollars," the Police Commissioner arrogantly corrected.

This discovery was the beginning of a long (and for me a bitter and financially unrewarding) war fought in hearing rooms, the courts, the press, on radio and television, and in union meetings. My reward was an inner feeling of restful

---

*Shakespeare (once convicted of poaching), Sonnet 66.

pride, for I had made it possible for principle to prevail, and thereby many thousands of livelihoods were made more secure and our musical and cultural arts enriched. Referred to as "The Police Card Cases," they are still regarded as a classical clinical study of police abuse, civil rights, and legal tactics.

Even though the Police Card problem was resolved, such fundamental threats, in one variable form or another, may well arise again. It is therefore incumbent upon me, as the proponent, to record the details of the battle, and its hopes, disappointments, failures, victories, tragedies, extraordinary climaxes, and ultimate solution which was so important to so many people.

* * *

The last two weeks of November and the first week of December 1960 were three of the strangest weeks in New York City's history. A noted monologist, Lord Buckley, denied a Police Card by the New York City Police Department for a minor offense committed almost two decades previously had died from malnutrition and a kidney ailment. More than seventy well-known writers, editors, publishers, entertainers, and public figures residing in New York City sparked the three weeks of activity immediately following Buckley's strange death.

A Citizens' Emergency Committee was formed to fight New York City's powerfully entrenched Police Department and to protect the employment rights of performers and rehabilitated criminals. A hearing was conducted by the Police Department to determine whether a cabaret employee's identification card should be granted by the police to a dead man, as demanded by his family. New York City's most powerful and much-publicized Police Commissioner, Stephen Kennedy, injected himself into that hearing to ridicule and attack the Citizens' Emergency Committee in front of television cameras, press photographers and reporters, and in turn was himself brutally deflated for almost six continuous hours while the television cameras recorded the scene. The Police Commissioner was dismissed and as a consequence of the hearing he was conclusively removed from consideration as President Kennedy's nominee to succeed J. Edgar Hoover as Director of the F.B.I.

New York's Governor, Nelson Rockefeller, almost became involved in what appeared to be a matter of international rather than local interest. It was revealed that Buckley had been invited to perform, free of charge, at a banquet of the Honor Society of the Police Department, where it was suggested that a bribe of $100 would obtain permission for him to work in New York City. The check was actually given while the distinguished group of police officers and their guests were celebrating. When the charge was made public, sufficient pressure was placed upon the bribe solicitor to deny the incident. The officers of several unions sided with the police, notwithstanding their members' opposition to the Police Card system.

An amazing climax of events, which terminated the Citizens' Emergency Committee, occurred when one of America's best known writers (and one of the leaders of the Committee) was arrested for stabbing his wife and another leader of the Committee, also a novelist, was jailed because he wanted to pay a traffic fine by check as he carried no cash with him.

But let us stop this breathless pace and proceed with more leisurely logic—from the beginning.

# CHAPTER ONE

"But that's the law" is the most familiar defense or explanation given to one who protests or rebels at an infringement of rights, liberty, and inherent privileges. We are conditioned to accept this explanation without further inquiry, and so to acquiesce in the continued abuse.

One unchallenged abuse to our rights is the inevitable prelude to other and continued infringements. A passive acquiescence to an abuse purportedly because "that's the law" ultimately solidifies what was initially no valid law but an unlawful arrogation of authority into a harsh reality.

I told editor Alan Morrison and Birdland manager Oscar Goodstein that my thorough search and investigation had clearly and conclusively shown that there was no explicit statutory authority which unequivocally gave the New York City Police Department the power to demand the acquisition of a Cabaret Employee's Identification Card from Bud Powell (or any other prospective employee) as a requisite for lawful employment in cabarets. Nor was there a statute which explicitly gave the Police Department the right and power to charge $2 as a "service charge" for a Cabaret Employee Identification Card; nor was there an explicit statute which unequivocally authorized the Police Department to place the monies so received into the Police Pension Fund, or the Police Pension Fund to receive and place such monies into its fund. In fact, the Police Department's assumption of the authority to bar rehabilitated employees (or other employees) was contrary to New York State public policy, as set forth in court decisions and legislation.

Morrison passed on that information to the editor of *Down*

1

*Beat,* a magazine for music lovers and jazz musicians, and Goodstein spread the news to jazz musicians.

It was not an objection to fingerprinting as such, as was suggested by way of oversimplification in Police Department press releases and in their Court Memoranda of Law. The applicant-employees must have been fingerprinted as infants, as military personnel, as USO performers, as participants in United States Cultural Exchange Programs, and in some states on automobile licenses.

The objection was to the unauthorized assertion by the Police Department of the power to regulate and control the cabaret employees' rights to lawful employment and to publicly regard these employees as a distinct and lower class of the entertainment industry, with accompanying derogatory and offensive overtones.*

Subsequently, several musicians and their attorneys called on me for advice and assistance in preparing applications or defending their rights to cards when applications were denied. In all these instances, I did not charge for advice and consultation. In the event a card was denied, I requested Police Department hearings and prepared Memoranda of Law, testimony of witnesses, affidavits, etc. If a musician or performer was unemployed, I would represent him at no charge. The Police Department knew this.

If the applicant could pay for legal services the fee charged was $350, no matter how high the applicant's income. This fee rarely paid for the stenographic and secretarial services required to prepare memoranda and affidavits, for my appearances at hearings, or for necessary interviews and conferences.

The Police Card Cases involved important legal and social issues. However, an introduction to some of the real and typical principals is appropriate in order to give emotional

---

*The further objections will be discussed in the course of this narrative.

depth, human substance, and identification to an otherwise impersonal chronicle of litigation.*

David Allen was a singer, recording artist, cabaret and television performer. In (or about) September 1958, the Leipzig Duane Corporation engaged him as a singer and entertainer for The Den, its restaurant-cabaret. Since Allen had been convicted of a crime in 1955, it was necessary for permission for such employment to be obtained, pursuant to the Alcoholic Beverage Control Law, from the New York State Liquor Authority. The New York City Police Department also required its approval or disapproval. Permission was granted by the State Liquor Authority.

The officers of the corporation knew that Allen was a former offender, but they also knew that, after his discharge from prison, he had perfected himself as an artist, had received additional medical treatment, and had become so thoroughly rehabilitated that many newspaper columnists, performers, and distinguished public figures had become his sponsors and friends. During the intervening years he had not violated any law and his stature as an artist and as a mature individual had been confirmed by frequent performance on radio and television, including several appearances on the Steve Allen Show, and by the success of his three LP recordings.

Meanwhile, Allen applied to the Division of Licenses of the Police Department for a Cabaret Employee's Identification Card. Letters supporting his application were sent to the Deputy Police Commissioner by prominent citizens and officials. The Department's attention was called to his history as a combat veteran awarded a Purple Heart. The Police Department refused to grant him employment permission. After this became known, two radio programs and several columnists conducted a public campaign on his behalf. The

---

*Identities in this book are matters of public record and press coverage, so the names of the principals can be properly used.

Deputy Police Commissioner remained adamant and refused to grant a Cabaret Employee's Identification Card.

Because Allen had appeared and performed at The Den without the Police Identification Card, the Police Department sent a communication to the Leipzig Duane Corporation on October 31, 1958, setting a hearing date for Tuesday, November 18 and directing the corporation "to show cause why its license should not be suspended or revoked" for employing Allen without a Cabaret Employee's Identification Card and for failing to record his name "in the Personnel Roster Book," and because they "did employ one David Allen, a known criminal."

Following the hearing on November 18 and 20, the plaintiff-corporation was notified that its Cabaret License was to be suspended for a three-day period, commencing on Thanksgiving Day, November 27, through November 29, 1958—three major income-producing days.

At the hearing on November 18, the Police Department's contention that Allen was a "known criminal" was challenged and fought, we thought, convincingly. The Police Hearing Office ruled that the allegation was not sustained. Notwithstanding the ruling that Allen was not a "known criminal," the Department still refused to grant him a Cabaret Employee's Identification Card.

* * *

Bill Rubenstein was a pianist. In 1951 and 1954, while attending Syracuse University, Bill was arrested and convicted for possession of marijuana. The Police Department was informed that Bill was 14 years old when his father, a federal official, was killed in action while on a combat mission in the Pacific. His mother never remarried. At Syracuse, where he was a music major, Bill became associated with a brilliant, if unstable, group of students and was exposed to marijuana, leading to two arrests and convictions. Some time after graduation from the University, he married a professional social worker, became a father, and most favorably adjusted his life.

At hearings conducted by the Police Department, reputable witnesses testified to Rubenstein's readjustment and rehabilitation. There was testimony concerning the hardships imposed on his wife and child because he had to leave them often to work outside of New York.

The Hearing Officer recommended a card. However, even before the minutes of the hearing were transcribed, the Deputy Police Commissioner, who had not participated in the hearing, overruled the Hearing Officer and denied Rubenstein a card.

The Kafkaesque quality of this case can best be depicted by quoting Paragraph Thirty-Fourth of our Supreme Court complaint when I instituted an action on his behalf, the first of our attacks on the Police Department. Law drafting permits this type of sentence structure:

THIRTY-FOURTH: The rejection by the Deputy Police Commissioner of the petition of the plaintiff, RUBENSTEIN, for a Cabaret Employee's Identification Card in evident disregard of the pre-emptive State Liquor Authority's permission granted to the plaintiff to accept work in New York City; his arbitrary refusal to accept the recommendation of his own Hearing Officer who had observed the plaintiff, RUBENSTEIN, his wife, a former Social Worker, and reputable character witnesses, and who had actively conducted and participated in the Hearing; the Deputy Commissioner's summarily denying the plaintiff a Cabaret Employee's Identification Card even before the Minutes of the Hearing conducted before the Hearing Officer were transcribed for his review; the delay by the Deputy Police Commissioner for over one month in reviewing the petition after the Hearing; the refusal of the Police Commissioner to accept the Appeal for review and his referral of the telegram and Appeal to the Deputy Police Commissioner, thus designating the Deputy

Police Commissioner as an Appellate Authority over his own decisions of denial; the Deputy Police Commissioner's improperly receiving as evidence untested confidential departmental reports by the Syracuse arresting officers, and his acceptance of the contents of these reports as true, notwithstanding the fact that the Syracuse police records were erroneous and obviously in conflict with the submitted Certified Copies of Disposition of the two arrests issued by the Court of Special Sessions of the City of Syracuse (Annexed hereto as Exhibit "D-[10–11]"), and the Minutes of the sentencing proceedings in Syracuse; the constant inquiry and references at the second Hearing to the plaintiff's traffic violations when these violations are specifically excluded from consideration by the Department of Licenses own form (See Exhibit "A"); the Deputy Police Commissioner's disregard of plaintiff, RUBENSTEIN's evidence of rehabilitation, marriage, parenthood and good employment records, all attested to by reputable witnesses; the indifference regarding the undeserved hardships resulting to the plaintiff's wife and new-born child living in New York City, as a result of the forced separation necessitated by the plaintiff, RUBENSTEIN's seeking employment, to support his family, outside of New York City; the refusal of the Police Commissioner of the City of New York to acknowledge or accept the Appeal for Review dated September 11, 1958, all of the foregoing constitutes unreasonable, oppressive, arbitrary and unconstitutional conduct and processes by the defendant, STEPHEN P. KENNEDY, as Police Commissioner of the City of New York and JAMES J. McELROY, as Deputy Police Commissioner of the City of New York in Charge of Licenses, to the detriment of and damage to the plaintiff, RUBENSTEIN.

\* \* \*

James Louis (J. J.) Johnson was a world-famous artist, winner of every single popularity poll as a master of his particular instrument, the trombone, in the past five years, performing for literally over 100,000,000 people a year, in all parts of the world, via personal appearances, radio and TV appearances, and recordings. He had committed a minor offense, a misdemeanor, in 1946—13 years prior to his application. There had been no other arrest or conviction since.

He was married, living with his wife and two children, owner of his own home and active in fraternal organizations. He had been denied a Cabaret Employee's Identification Card consistently, until about November 1956, at which time he was given a Temporary Card conditioned upon his bringing proof from a City hospital that he was not a narcotics addict. (He never was a narcotics addict.)

No New York City hospital then had facilities to conduct such examinations, nor were they permitted to conduct such examinations by the Mental Hygiene Law. The Police Department was informed of this. Johnson was then told to present a doctor's certificate every six months for his Temporary Card.

On June 12, 1958, he was told by the new Deputy Police Commissioner, James J. McElroy, that he would only be given a card restricted to a particular place of employment, and this only providing he obtained certification from a City hospital.

Johnson was unable to accept any cabaret engagements because of the practical impossibility of constantly applying to a New York City hospital for an examination which the hospital could not conduct by law, and for certification of nonaddiction from a City hospital as a condition precedent to the issuance of a Temporary Card which, even if granted, would restrict him only to a particular and designated cabaret for employment.

The deliberate and callous brutality of this system can best be shown by Rubenstein's and Johnson's allegations in the complaint—none of which were denied by the Police.

THIRTY-EIGHTH: Plaintiff, JOHNSON, at all times here-inafter mentioned was and is a Musician by training, skill and profession.

THIRTY-NINTH: On December 27, 1946, plaintiff, JOHNSON, was arrested on a misdemeanor, convicted and received a suspended sentence. This was and is his only arrest.

There has been no other arrest within the past eleven years, or since December, 1946.

FORTIETH: Prior to October, 1956, plaintiff, JOHNSON, had made several applications to the Division of Licenses for a Permanent Cabaret Employee's Identification Card, but these applications had been denied. No reason was stated.

FORTY-FIRST: On or about October 22, 1956, plaintiff, JOHNSON, renewed his Application and Appeal. Formally and informally the Division of Licenses was informed.

(a) That plaintiff, JOHNSON, had been arrested only once, in 1946;

(b) That he has been continuously married since 1947; that he had two children; that he owned his own home; that he was a member in good standing of fraternal organizations;

(c) That he enjoyed world wide prestige as a trombonist, conductor, composer and was under exclusive contract with Columbia Records as a Recording Artist;

(d) That during the past five years, plaintiff, JOHNSON, had been voted first place as the most outstanding trombone performer by all Critics Polls, Magazine Polls, Trade Polls and Popularity Polls;

(e) That because of television performances, radio performances, concert appearances, cabaret performances, record sales and performances both in the United States and throughout the world, plaintiff, JOHNSON, has been heard and is heard by many millions of listeners;

(f) That in his public appearances and performances before college audiences, adult audiences, groups of all ages, both in the United States and the other countries in the world, plaintiff, JOHNSON, was and is publicly accepted and acknowledged as a representative American Negro Artist and a typical American family man and as evidence of the fact that racial strife is not typical of United States culture;

(g) That, upon information and belief, at no time was public safety, community mores, or the individual listener's social behavior adversely affected or influenced by plaintiff JOHNSON's appearances or performance as an artist in any part of the world; and

(h) That plaintiff, JOHNSON's performances in New York Cabarets did not constitute a public threat or menace to public safety any more than his performances in the larger New York theatres, concert halls and television studios.

FORTY-SECOND: The Application for a Cabaret Employee's Identification Card, was, nevertheless, denied by the Police Department of the City of New York. No reason was stated, despite the overwhelming and conclusive proof of the plaintiff, JOHNSON's character, and the international prestige which he has earned.

FORTY-THIRD: The State Liquor Authority, in the interim, had favorably ruled that there would be no need hereafter for the plaintiff, JOHNSON, to apply to the State Liquor Authority for permission to work in New York, and dispensed with the need for further Applications.

FORTY-FOURTH: Plaintiff, JOHNSON, then requested by telegram, a Hearing from the then Deputy Police Commissioner in Charge of the Division of Licenses. The Hearing was denied, but on November 7, 1956, the plaintiff was then informed by the then Deputy Police Commissioner in Charge of the Division of Licenses that he would receive a six months Temporary Card, and upon completing a condition, a Permanent Card would be considered.

The following letter was sent by the Deputy Police Commissioner to the plaintiff, JOHNSON, through his attorney:

(SEAL)
POLICE DEPARTMENT
City of New York
New York 13, N.Y.

November 7, 1956

Mr. Maxwell T. Cohen
Attorney of Law
505 Fifth Avenue
New York, New York

*Re. James L. Johnson*

Dear Mr. Cohen:

With reference to your telegram of November 2nd, 1956, concerning the issuance of a Cabaret Employee's I.D. Card to the abovementioned applicant, kindly be informed that I have completed my review of the matter and I have ordered that a six months temporary I.D. Card be issued to Mr. Johnson. He is to submit a statement from any New York City Hospital at the end of this six month period, indicating that he has been examined thereat and was found to be free of narcotic use. If after this period there is no further criminal involvement we will consider the issuance of a permanent I.D. Card, provided, of course, that he has clearance from the State Liquor Authority.

Very truly yours,
(SIGNED) ROBERT J. MANGUM
Deputy Commissioner
Licenses & Juvenile Aid

FORTY-FIFTH: That plaintiff, JOHNSON, is not now and never was a narcotic addict.

FORTY-SIXTH: The then Deputy Police Commissioner was informed by the plaintiff, JOHNSON, through his attorney, that no New York City Hospital could conduct, or had the facilities to conduct, the examination requested to determine whether an individual was free from narcotic use.

FORTY-SEVENTH: It was then suggested that the

plaintiff, JOHNSON, at the end of the six months period, supply certification by a reputable physician.

FORTY-EIGHTH: Plaintiff, JOHNSON, in pursuance of the aforementioned letter, and at the end of the six months period, did present certification from a reputable physician. A Permanent Card was denied him. No reason was stated.

FORTY-NINTH: Plaintiff, JOHNSON, at the termination of every subsequent six month interval, renewed his Application for a Permanent Cabaret Employee's Identification Card, presented his medical evidence but was, nevertheless, denied a Permanent Card. He was instead issued a Temporary Card.

FIFTIETH: The State Liquor Authority, in the interim, had favorably ruled that there would be no need hereafter for the plaintiff, JOHNSON, to apply to the State Liquor Authority for permission to work in New York State, or New York City, and dispensed with the need for further applications.

FIFTY-FIRST: In the interim, the present Deputy Police Commissioner, JAMES J. MCELROY, was appointed Deputy Police Commissioner in Charge of the Division of Licenses, replacing the former Deputy Police Commissioner, ROBERT J. MANGUM.

FIFTY-SECOND: On June 12, 1958, plaintiff, JOHNSON, appeared at the Division of Licenses, at No. 156 Greenwich Street, New York City, with a doctor's certificate. He submitted his request for a Permanent Card and annexed thereto his doctor's certificate. The Officer in Charge then made several statements, the substance of which is herein presented:

That there were changes made in the policy; and that he had no authority to issue a Temporary Card; and that the plaintiff, JOHNSON, was to see the Deputy Police Commissioner at once.

FIFTY-THIRD: Plaintiff, JOHNSON, was on the aforementioned date interviewed by the Deputy Police Commissioner. Plaintiff, JOHNSON, was told in substance, by the Deputy Police Commissioner, that there are now "new policies"; new restrictions; that doctor's certificates would not be acceptable; that plaintiff, JOHNSON, would have to report to any New York City Hospital for an examination, and then obtain a certificate from the Hospital that he was not addicted to drugs; that upon doing so, a Temporary Card would be issued to him, but that the Card would restrict the plaintiff, JOHNSON, only to a particular and specific place of employment.

FIFTY-FOURTH: Upon information and belief, the New York City Hospitals are specifically prevented by policy from accepting narcotic addict patients except if they suffer withdrawal symptoms in conjunction with any other ailment, and this prohibition has been extended to the extreme where New York City Hospitals refuse to examine any person for the purposes of ascertaining and certifying whether or not the individual is addicted.

FIFTY-FIFTH: Upon information and belief, the Division of Licenses of the Police Department knows, and has been informed, that no New York City Hospital will examine any applicant with a view of certifying whether or not he is addicted to the use of narcotics.

FIFTY-SIXTH: (a) Upon information and belief, the Police Department's Representative, JOSEPH L. COYLE, Deputy Chief Inspector commanding its narcotic squad, testified at Public Hearings conducted by the State of New York Joint Legislative Committee on Narcotic Study.

(b) Upon information and belief, in the widely distributed Second Interim Report of the State of New York Joint Legislative Committee on Narcotic Study (Legislative Document 1958, No. 16, dated February 10, 1958), in which reference is made to the testimony of the Police Department's Representative and other City Officials, the Legislative Committee reported (page 25):

"Commissioner Morris Jacobs of the New York City Department of Hospitals, testified before the committee that there are no facilities for adults, except '* * * when individuals present themselves to our other institutions with extreme withdrawal symptoms and possible complications of other conditions like diabetes or nephritis, in addition to the drug addiction, we admit these people and take care of their conditions.' Dr. Jacobs agreed that the general policy of the hospital system'* * * is not to extend facilities for care or treatment of narcotic addicts.' This policy has been established, according to the Commissioner, because of personnel shortages, lack of space, pressures for treatment of patients with other diseases where prognosis is more hopeful, lack of medical agreement on the optimum treatment for narcotic addicts, sociological components of the narcotic problem, and many other reasons."

FIFTY-SEVENTH: Upon information and belief, the Division of Licenses of the Police Department notwithstanding this knowledge, nevertheless deliberately demanded that plaintiff, JOHNSON, and other applicants obtain such impossible examination and certification from any New York City Hospital as a means of discouraging an Application for a Cabaret Employee's Identification Card by any applicant who had ever been convicted of any narcotic offense, no matter how remote in time.

FIFTY-EIGHTH: Plaintiff, JOHNSON, when interviewed by the Deputy Police Commissioner, was engaged to perform at "Small's Paradise" for one week and was, therefore, restricted to that place of employment by the Temporary Employee's Identification Card (See Exhibit "L").

FIFTY-NINTH: Plaintiff, JOHNSON's services were requested by "Birdland," "Village Vanguard," "Cafe Bohemia," "The Continental," and other well known Cabarets. Plaintiff, JOHNSON, was unable to accept any of the aforementioned engagements because of the practical impossibility of constantly applying to any New York City Hospital for an examination which

could not be conducted, for certification which could
not be issued, as a condition precedent to the issuance
of a Temporary Card which even, if granted, would
restrict him only to a particular and designated cabaret
for employment.

SIXTIETH: Because of the oppressive, unconstitutional
and unlawful proceedings by the Division of Licenses,
as aforementioned, plaintiff, JOHNSON, is excluded from
performing in cabarets in New York City and from
engaging other musicians to perform with him in the
Cabarets in New York City.

These cases were typical. (The Lord Buckley case, the
most publicized, will be discussed in Chapter Six.) Multiply
them by thousands of other applicants whose applications
were denied. Now consider once again the consequences of
the denials on the applicants' wives, children, and employment opportunities.

In applying for a card, the applicant was required to
complete a form, to be fingerprinted and to supply a small
photo. Although there was no inquiry made in the form as to
whether the applicant was ever convicted of any felony or
misdemeanor or offense, the applicant was asked

    7. (a) Were you ever arrested or summoned (except
         traffic violation). (Yes or No _____)
      (b) If answer is Yes, state how many times and give
         facts _____.

Thus, in absolute violation of all known and accepted
constitutional and statutory laws, an arrest, which per se is no
evidence of guilt, was improperly and unlawfully made
equivalent to a conviction of crime by the Police Department, a situation detrimental to the applicant and prejudicial
to his right to obtain lawful employment.

If the application indicated that the applicant was ever
"arrested" or convicted, then, in accordance with the usual
and established procedure of the Division of Licenses, the

applicant was then and there told or "advised" by an officer on duty not to submit his application, for the consequence of such submission would be a denial. Tens of thousands of prospective employees were thus deprived of the right to work.

If the applicant insisted upon submitting his application, in spite of this "advice" not to, and in addition supplied corroborative evidence of rehabilitation and/or of good reputation and character, or a State Liquor Authority Employment permission, such application was then reviewed by a higher officer for denial or approval at a later date—often too late for the specific employment possibility—or for a scheduled hearing by the Division of Licenses.

These hearings were at first conducted alongside a desk, were very brisk and routine, and inevitably resulted in a denial. Fortunately, later two of the finest men I have known, Deputy Inspector Francis Lent and Captain James O'Rourke, were transferred to the License Division. In any large force such as the New York City Police Department, men of integrity are usually considered odd and are hidden away, like demented relatives, in corners. Inspector Lent and Captain O'Rourke were thus exiled to this troublesome branch of the Police Department.

Although it was not incumbent upon them to do so, Inspector Lent and Captain O'Rourke transferred the hearings from their unsympathetic subordinates and assumed the responsibility of conducting them.

The hearings were conducted with the solemnity of Supreme Court trials. The Police Department was represented by an officer, usually a lawyer on the force, who opposed the granting of the card. I presented a prepared memorandum of law. Affidavits were necessary. Character witnesses and members of the family were called. Mine was the burden of proving the good character and reputation of the applicant, while at the same time I challenged the jurisdiction of the Police Department. I was always granted full opportunity to present my case by Inspector Lent or Captain O'Rourke.

Inspector Lent was a very tall, taciturn career man. He was deeply religious. Following his retirement, he became an official for an interfaith movement. Unfortunately, he died while serving this cause.

Captain O'Rourke was a scholar, with the ascetic appearance of a priest and the quiet smile of a man at peace with himself and the world. One day, he made a literary reference while speaking with me; he could not remember the author. Over the weekend, I discovered the source of the quotation and informed him of my finding in a letter which was mailed that Monday. That very same day, before he received my letter, he phoned my office and left word that he had discovered the source of the quotation.

These were the gentlemen who now conducted hearings. Unfortunately, the Police Commissioner, observing that cards were being granted after hearings, directed the Deputy Police Commissioner in charge of the Department of Licenses to review the decisions of Lent and O'Rourke. In every instance, the Deputy Commissioner overruled the decision of the hearing officer, or granted conditional cards if certain requirements were met. As in the Johnson case, these requirements were often impossible to fulfill and were almost certainly known by the Deputy Commissioner to be impossible.

# CHAPTER TWO

The genesis of any violation of rights is interesting—and strange. The Police Department's violation of employment rights was born in hypocrisy and lawlessness, then assumed a new role as a political security check, and finally was nurtured into a censorial reality affecting employment rights—far removed from its initial purpose.

The courts have held that in construing a statute it is relevant to consider the history of the times, the circumstances surrounding the passage of the statute, the mischief felt, and the objects and remedy in view (*People v. Jelke,* 284 A.D. 211, 308, N.Y. 56).

On June 17, 1926, in the Board of Estimate and Apportionment, a local law "to regulate dance halls and cabarets" was introduced by Mayor James J. Walker. Section 4 of that law placed the power to license cabarets with the *Commissioner of Licenses*—not the Police Commissioner.

There was no reference to employees in the bill; *cabarets* required licenses. There were no provisions pertaining to employees. This statute defined a cabaret as follows:

> 3. The word "cabaret" shall mean any room, place or space in the city in which any musical entertainment, singing, dancing or other similar amusement is permitted in connection with the restaurant business or the business of directly or indirectly selling to the public food or drink. (§1 subdivision 3)

Prohibition, the Eighteenth Amendment of the United States Constitution, was then the law of the land and as such binding upon New York City and its officials. Seemingly paradoxical, then, was this statute which placed under supervision of the Commissioner of Licenses of the City of New York, and later the Police Commissioner, a facility or enterprise only violating the law, the speakeasy "directly or indirectly selling to the public food or drink."

The new and amended license provisions which transferred authority to the Police Commissioner applied only to cabarets *and not to employees*. The definition of the cabaret remained the same.

Although the Eighteenth Amendment was still the law of the land, the statute was made more farcical, if somewhat more colorful, by the fact that the law-breaking enterprise was now under the supervision of the Police Commissioner. The speakeasy still "directly or indirectly selling the public food or drink" had to qualify and pay license fees to the Police Commissioner, the very official whose function it presumably was to apprehend and prosecute the law-breaker.

The Seabury Vice Inquiry on February 25, 1932 disclosed that many men still on the police force were either active or silent partners in thousands of speakeasies. On that very same day, there was a Police Department hearing involving Patrolmen Quinlaven and O'Connor. According to press reports, they were accused of hiring a collector, Levey, who collected $7,500 for them each and every month from 150 speakeasies.

On October 1, 1940, *14 years after* the initial statute, supervising the employer-enterprise, *nine years after* the amended statute, and *three years after* the statutes were incorporated in the City Charter and the Administrative Code, the Police Commissioner created—*not* by statute or by ordinance or by legislative authority—the rules and regulations providing control over *employees* by means of the unlawful and oppressive Cabaret Employee Identification Card.

Actually the cabaret police card came into existence for completely different reasons not related to crime prevention or control.

A study of strikes and labor difficulties of that period is revealing. The Brass Rail Restaurants in 1940 had had a waiters' strike in progress for almost four continuous years. Waiters and chefs were on strike against Schraffts, Childs, Toots Shor, the Stork Club and every major restaurant chain in the City of New York. The restaurants serving visitors at the World's Fair were threatened with strikes.

It was believed, and evidently with some accuracy, that the Joint Board of Waiters and Chefs was Communist-dominated.

Cabaret Employee Identification Card rules and regulations were first applied to the chefs and waiters. (It is important to note that they were not applied to musicians until about two years later. Nor were they initially applied to performers, cashiers, porters, or any other restaurant help.)

In the first and leading case on Police Cards, *Friedman v. Valentine,* the petitioners were several labor unions whose members were employed in hotels, restaurants, and cabarets as chefs, waiters, and bartenders. The pleadings indicated, as the opinion partially confirms, that the prime concern of the unions involved was the issue of fingerprinting and certain violations of labor rights, and, inferentially, that due to the climate of that time (1939–1941) the Police Department's newly innovated procedures of registration and fingerprinting were politically undemocratic procedures.

In the petitioner Friedman's Brief, page 31, it was stated:

> In this connection, we respectfully urge upon the Court the fact that fingerprinting and identification cards are part of an internal passport system which does not comport with the American way of life, and which infringes upon the fundamental rights of liberty which only the sovereign state, acting under the police power, may abrogate for good cause shown.

The petitioners contended (Paragraph 24 of Friedman Petition) that there were in fact no incidents of crime or conditions of crimes in the cabaret industry. They inferred that the newly established Rules and Regulations (June 20, 1940) was a ruse to prepare a labor black-list and a means to bar union organizers from the field of operations. In short, it was alleged that the Rules and Regulations were politically motivated and not a crime deterrent.

On September 6, 1939, President Roosevelt announced the F.B.I.'s broadened responsibility for national security. F.B.I. chief J. Edgar Hoover stated:

> . . . when this work was assigned to us we organized . . . the Central Intelligence Division, which will have supervision of espionage, sabotage, and other subversive activities, and violations of the neutrality regulations. . . . We have also initiated special investigations of persons reported upon as being active in any subversive activity or in movements detrimental to the internal security. In that connection, we have a general index, arranged alphabetically and geographically, available at the Bureau, so that in the event of any greater emergency coming to our country we will be able to locate immediately these various persons who may need to be the subject of further investigation . . .

On June 20, 1940, Police Commissioner Valentine promulgated the original Rules and Regulations of the Division of Licenses, directing these Rules specifically, it was charged, at hotel, restaurant, and cabaret employees who were, because of their employment, members of the suspect unions. The Police Commissioner denied that the Rules and Regulations were politically motivated. Four weeks later, Pearl Harbor was bombed, and the question of political motivation became unimportant.

It is interesting to note from the news item in the *New York Times* which reported *Friedman v. Valentine* that on the

argument of the motion, the Justice presiding indicated that
the police regulations were "too broad." There was discussion with Assistant Corporation Counsel Weinstein as to
whether the word "record" meant criminal record. The
Judge further said "there is a serious question as to whether
some of the regulations contravene fundamental rights."

There was no hearing or trial in the *Friedman* case. It was
decided on affidavits. Although the burden of proving
necessity and justification is—and should be—properly
placed on the Police Department, the Court's opinion
alleged that "Petitioners have failed to show that the
regulations under attack are not justified by conditions
existing in the cabaret industry." The petitioners were the
Joint Board of Waiters & Chefs.

The Police Department's affidavits, presumably the basis
for that decision since there was no hearing, warrant
consideration.

The Police Department submitted three affidavits in its
defense. There was an affidavit by Commissioner Valentine
containing a learned discussion on the history of fingerprinting, a defense of fingerprinting, and a few uncomplimentary
opinions on cabarets. The burden of the Police Department's
defense was borne by Lt. Thomas P. McLaughlin and
Detective Thomas P. Tunney.

Lt. McLaughlin's contributions, when stripped of opinions
and irrelevancies, demonstrably showed that cabarets were,
in fact, relatively well-conducted institutions. In a 5-year
period, a total of 6,571 licenses were issued. There were only
26 revocations, a better record of good conduct than the
much-investigated Police Department.

Detective Tunney's contribution consisted of several well-
written stories on jewel thefts. He was hard pressed,
however, to relate the jewel robberies to cabarets and
cabaret employees. None took place in cabarets. Those
robbed had worn jewels to parties, functions, etc.

On Page 3 of Detective Tunney's affidavit is an example of
the heroic struggle to relate cabarets and cabaret employees

to the evil graphically denounced by the learned Court in *Matter of Friedman v. Valentine*. He writes: "Dolly Turner . . . possessed some knowledge as to the value of jewelry, she made a practice of visiting night clubs, accompanied by 'Pick,' in an effort to pick out promising victims for the ring."

Neither of these Dickensian-named characters, "Dolly Turner" and "Pick," were cabaret employees—but patrons.

To the reader who survived this litany of illogic and the succeeding nine pages, Detective Tunney then presented the coup de grace to sanity, logic, and sense of reality with this display—quoted verbatim, but with emphasis added (p. 12):

> Although the investigations conducted in connection with the robberies described above did *not yield evidence* of sufficient weight directly *to implicate employees of the various cabarets* involved, circumstances were discovered in various instances which justified an *inference* that the operations of the ring were facilitated by cooperation on the part of such employees. Such *inference is fortified by the fact that Dolly Turner, who constantly frequented night clubs and was the acting link between the ring and such establishments, has never cooperated with the law enforcement authorities and has never disclosed the information in her possession as to the operations of the ring.*

On this foundation, the civil rights and employment opportunities of thousands of men and women were unlawfully destroyed.

There were several irregularities in the Court procedures sufficient to offset the aroma of sanctimony which distorted the issues in that case. *Friedman v. Valentine* was to haunt almost every attempt to fight the Card system.

In order to apply to the New York State Supreme Court for a review of an administrative proceeding decision of any city or state agency, one must exhaust all the appellate remedies available within that agency. I appealed the denials by telegrams to New York City's Police Commissioner. He never acknowledged the telegrams and thus made it possible for me to move on the first of many cases attacking the Police Card System in the New York State Supreme Court.

# CHAPTER THREE

We were now ready to proceed for a test case in the New York State Supreme Court.

I knew by this time that I had infuriated the Police Department and some areas of the city administration. I also knew of the legitimate resources of the Police Department—its experienced staff of departmental lawyers and also the staff of the New York City Law Department—as well as what may be referred to as the Department's illegitimate resources—its great power, which would leave many judges reluctant to sit impartially on this explosive case.

I had no legal assistants available to me. However, as an experienced attorney, I knew that thorough preparation in every aspect of this case would place me on a militant parity with the accumulated staffs and resources of the Police Department and the city.

The Police Department's answer admitted for the first time that there was no explicit authority with regard to the Police Cards and for the imposition of fees and the deposit of such funds in the Police Pension Fund. The answer did assert, however, that the authority was implied in the power of the Police Commissioner to make reasonable rules and regulations.

What constitutes reasonable rules and regulations is determined by conditions and circumstances. It was therefore necessary for me to prepare my case by reviewing the history of the police authority with respect to Police Cards, and the Constitutional and social principles involved. I based my case on several legal and social principles, which may be summarized as follows:

*One:* The creation of rules relating to Police Cards by the Police Commissioner was an assertion by him of sovereign legislative power not authorized by statute. He was exceeding the proper limitations of delegated administrative power. He was intruding into an area not intended by the Legislature—the power to preclude lawful employment by certain individuals. Therefore the pertinent, strict rules of construction should warrant the Court's condemnation of the Police Department's Division of Licenses Rules and Regulations as unlawful, improper, and therefore void as they pertained to cabarets, hotels, restaurants, and cabaret employees.

Had it been the legislative intent to confer such powers or any regulatory power over cabaret *employees* or the right to establish qualifications or disqualifications for employees seeking lawful employment in cabarets, the Legislature would have done so. It would have outlined legislative policy, fixed controlling general principles, created adequate standards, and then delegated the authority to administer to the Police Department.

The legislative intent was patently to create supervision over cabarets only (cf. "cabaret" defined, "cabaret" fees fixed, etc.) and not over present or prospective cabaret employees seeking lawful employment.

*Two:* The plaintiff applicants were deprived of property without due process of law.

The rights of Rubenstein, Johnson, Allen, and others to lawfully exercise their skills for compensation, the rights of Leipzig Duane Corp. to freely and lawfully employ others, were property rights in all respects when viewed from the viewpoint of legal and philosophical standards and principles.

Locke, in *Civil Government* (Chap. V), wrote: "For this labor, being the unquestionable property of the laborer. . . ." Shylock, in Shakespeare's *Merchant of Venice,* says: ". . .you take my life,/when you do take the means whereby I live" (act 4, scene 1).

In the preface to the published *Proceedings of the Academy of Political Science* (Vol. XXVI, No. 1, May 1954) Prof. Dumas Malone wrote: "Man's right to work is as incontestable as his other historical rights—such as freedom of speech and religion."

The right to work, the right to employ, is a property right. Our competitive economic system of free enterprise permits one to earn wages (profit), an economic factor, in exchange for the rendition of skilled services (labor), an economic factor. Our society permits, encourages, and approves the lawful exchange of services, abilities, and skills for proper compensation and gain. The concept of property is therefore based upon interrelationship of economic factors, i.e., the exchange of one consideration for another.

In *Smith v. Texas,* 233 U.S. 630, Justice Lamar stated:

> 1. Life, liberty, property and the equal protection of the law, grouped together in the Constitution, are so related that the deprivation of any one of those separate and independent rights may lessen or extinguish the value of the other three. In so far as a man is deprived of the right to labor his liberty is restricted, his capacity to earn wages and acquire property is lessened, and he is denied the protection when the law affords those who are permitted to work. Liberty means more than freedom from servitude, and the constitutional guaranty is an assurance that the citizen shall be protected in the right to use his powers of mind and body in any lawful calling (pp. 953–54).

*Three:* The individual's right to approved relationship with his family and community was also a property right if he conformed to the mores and ethics of Society. When one is a member of Society moving in that system, his right to belong, to be accepted, to conform, to function, and to contribute, is a property right. Whether a property right was corporeal or material or a conceptual civil right, the individual's retention of that right could not be diminished or confiscated without due process of law; that is the law of civilization, not the law of the jungle.

Ralph Waldo Emerson, in his *Essay on Politics,* wrote: "A man has a right to be employed, to be trusted, to be loved, to be revered."

*Four:* To exile one perpetually for an offense once committed and paid for, to stigmatize one and condemn one as "unclean" and "unfit" to associate with one's fellows for offenses once committed in the past, is to deprive one of status in the community, the right to participate in its needs, functions, and responsibilities. The status of communal approval and acceptance must be recognized as a property right in our complex but highly developed free Society.

Rubenstein, Johnson, Allen and thousands of other applicants who were denied Cards, sought status, sought security, sought to contribute their unique talents to a good society. The Police Department, without authority, scornfully condemned them, decreed them to be "unclean and unfit to work with one's fellows" and thus deprived them of status in their community, of their prime function as breadwinners for their families, of their public function as artists adding music, beauty, and pleasure to their fellow-men.

> *In the Matter of the Application of Fred H. Stubbe et al., Copartners, under the name of the Bronx Garage, Appellants, v. Robert Adamson et al., Constituting the Board of Hazardous Trades of the City of New York, Respondents,* 220 N.Y. 459, Hiscock, Ch. J.—the opinion read:

>> There must be a real evil, reasonably to be anticipated and to be guarded against, and if it appears from the face of the statute interpreted in the light of common knowledge that there is no evil or that there is no reasonable relation between the evil and the proposed remedy, or that the latter is unduly oppressive and confiscatory, the courts may

pronounce the legislation unconstitutional and re-
strain its enforcement. (*People v. Charles Schwein-
ler Press,* 214 N.Y. 395, 496, 407).

A right to reform is a basic essence of our Judeo-Christian
ethics and religions, indeed all religions and ethical move-
ments, and of our American judicial system.

The New York Court of Appeals in *People v. Pieri,* 269
N.Y. 315, 323, 327, Crane Ch. J. stated:

> We would never go so far I am sure as to say that
> because a man had been in prison he remained a
> criminal all his life. Some men, as we know, with no
> criminal propensities at all, have made mistakes, been
> overtaken by temptation, and paid the penalty the state
> demands. We would not add to their burden by saying
> or even intimating that they should be shunned or
> classed as criminals. . . .
>
> Persons who have been convicted of crimes and
> served the sentence imposed are not thereafter barred
> from society or intercourse with other human beings;
> they are not outcasts, nor to be treated as such. The
> legislature did not intend to close the doors to reforma-
> tion, repentance, or a new try at life. . . .

And in a more recent case, the same point of view was
re-expressed in 2 Miscellaneous Reports, 2d Series, 133, *In
The Matter of Nellie A. Tanner, Petitioner, against Carmine
G. DeSapio, as Secretary of State, Respondent,* Supreme
Court, Special Term, Cayuga County, March 19, 1956,
Arthur E. Blauvelt, J.

> However, the court refuses to subscribe to any
> philosophy that assumes that a person once dishonest
> may not by future conduct acquire good moral character.
> If such be the case, the State should alter its programs
> now in force in correctional institutions whereby refor-
> mation of convicts is undertaken. The duty of respondent

in the instant case was to determine whether or not the applicant was of good moral character at the time she applied for the licenses (p. 133).

A rationale of our position, and certainly of the humane values of correctional procedures now evident in many of our states, is stated in *Malvin v. Reid,* 112 Cal. App. 385, 397, Pac. 91 (1931):

> One of the major objectives of society as it is now constituted, and of the administration of our penal system, is the rehabilitation of the fallen and the reformation of the criminal. Under these theories of sociology it is our object to lift up and sustain the unfortunate rather than tear him down. Where a person has by his own efforts rehabilitated himself, we, as right-thinking members of society, should permit him to continue in the path of rectitude rather than throw him back into a life of shame or crime. . . . (112 C.A. at 292, 297 Pac. at 93).

*Five:* An improper imposition of an alleged "service charge" and the collection of such fees without authorization of law by a Municipal Agency deprives one of property without due process of law.

*Six:* In the absence of statutory authority, the burden of showing necessity and justification for the exercise of "police power" is upon the agency of Government—here, the Police Department—asserting that power.

*Seven:* Official action, whether or not based on statute, violates the requirement of due process if it comes within the judicial condemnation of arbitrariness.

*Eight:* If, as in the instant case, the designated officials act arbitrarily or capriciously, and if the conduct of the officials is predicated on unlawful assumption of authority, and if the very assumption of power by the officials is itself arbitrary and capricious, and if "their action was without adequate determining principle or was unreasoned" (to use the standard of Burton J., *United States v. Camick*, 329 U.S. 230, p. 243) then there is an outrage perpetrated on the due process concept and such conduct merits judicial condemnation.

*Nine:* Police Card requirements of the Division of Licenses of the Police Department were invalid because they were in conflict with the controlling and preeminent authority granted to the State Liquor Authority by the Legislature under the Alcoholic Beverage Control Law, with regard to employment by State Liquor Authority licensees of those formerly convicted of specifically designated crimes.

*Ten:* The unlawful assumption of authority, by the Police Department, was in violation of provisions of the Constitution of the State of New York and the Constitution of the United States of America in that the Police Department, constituted as a Penal Law Enforcement Agency of Government, violated the prohibition against ex post facto laws by adding to the original sentence of criminal conviction of an applicant for a Cabaret Employee's Identification Card, a punishment not contemplated by the Legislature—the deprivation of the lawful right to seek gainful employment after expiation of the charged offense.

*Eleven:* The overwhelming common law fundamental principle "that one is presumed innocent until proven guilty" negates any assumption or attribution of present unproven guilt, and rejects any concept which holds that a once expiated offense carries with it a status of criminal permanency, to be accepted as a presently existing criminal status and to be projected as a future criminal status. Therefore, the Police Department's unauthorized and assumed power to bar from lawful employment former but rehabilitated offenders was in derogation of their common law and constitutional rights and is unlawful.

*Twelve:* The Police Department's restriction of constitutional rights might be conceivably justified by the Police Department on the assumption that "convicted persons" are more likely than the population in general to commit crimes. A similar assumption might be made with respect to indigents with at least as much plausibility, and yet *Edwards v. California,* 314 U.S. 160, established that the status of indigents cannot be a basis for their deprivation of constitutional rights. Likewise, there may be statistical evidence that the crime rate among blacks and Puerto Ricans was higher in New York City than that for the population as a whole (see 27 F.B.I. Unif. Crime Report, 113 [1956]; Sutherland, *Principles of Criminology* 138–143, Ed. 1955, and New York crime reports), but it is apparent that blacks and Puerto Ricans should not be barred from employment or required to obtain Cards from the Police Department on that basis. The State's statutory power to prevent convicted persons from practicing medicine, law, holding public office, or even from voting, cannot justify or support the Police Department's Rules and Regulations that penalized a present innocent and passive status.

*Thirteen:* The right to adjust, the right to work which was violated by the Cabaret Card requirements of the Division of Licenses Rules and Regulations, was not merely an abstract right which was being abrogated. On the contrary, it hit the former offender where it hurt him most—in the blunt, pointed, often hostile reminder by the police of his past, and by the vindictive attitude that the past is not past, "once a criminal always a criminal." The consequences of this attitude were disastrous to the rehabilitation effort.

James V. Bennett, as Director of Federal Bureau of Prisons, wrote:

It has been my policy as Director of the Federal Bureau of Prisons not to disclose information which would identify any living individual as a former inmate of our prison system, if there is any possibility it might harm him. *If he has rehabilitated himself it is especially important that nothing be done to discourage him or thwart his efforts to adjust in the community* . . . . [emphasis added].

A similar view has been expressed by Austin N. Mac-Cormick, Professor of Criminology, University of California:

Under present penal and correctional methods in the United States, *a very substantial percentage of our ex-prisoners are rehabilitated, do not again revert to crime, and become respectable citizens.* The will to accomplish this rehabilitation, with the stigma of the ex-convict working against one at every turn, rests in large part on the belief that *it is possible to live down a criminal record by years of law-abiding life* . . . . (Id. at 102) [emphasis added].

*Fourteen:* The unlawful imposition of a "service charge" was an attack on due process and violation of Public Officers Law Sections 67 and 68, which prohibited unauthorized collections, tips, fees, and gifts.

*Fifteen:* In the instant case there was no statutory authority for the imposition of the so-called "service charge." The Police Department had assumed a sovereign authority in fixing such a "service charge" and in justifying this procedure by the assertion that it cost the City much more to render the service than was received from the $2.00 service charge. The irony of this defense was the fact that the money collected was not even given to the City, but was deposited in the Police Pension Fund—without authority of law.

*Sixteen:* The Card procedure flaunted New York State Court-declared public policy. In *People v. Pieri,* 269 N.Y. 315, Ch. J. Crane stated:

> Persons who have been convicted of crimes and served the sentence imposed are not thereafter barred from society or intercourse with other human beings; they are not outcasts, nor to be treated as such. The legislature did not intend to close the doors to reformation, repentance, or a new try at life. . . .

The communal right of the individual, his free choice and determination to be right, and the exertion of will to do right are much too important to him, to his family, to our system of jurisprudence, and to the community to be left to the mercy of the capricious, arbitrary whim and socially distorted viewpoint of officials who assume such power in the absence of statute and in violation of Constitutional rights and guarantees.

In no New York State statute or law is there a definition of the noun "criminal." Nevertheless, the Police Department's published Rules and Procedures supplied a barbaric and dangerous concept of that purported status.

*Ballantine's Law Dictionary* defines the word:

> In the eyes of the law, a person is a criminal who has been adjudged guilty of a crime, and he continues to be a criminal so long as the judgment remains in force.

When the "judgment is no longer in force," a person is no longer a criminal! When that person sought, as in these instant cases, a new status and a new adjustment by attempting to gain these ends by work, he was following Carlyle's observation: "Work is the grand cure of all maladies and miseries that ever beset mankind."

The Memorandum of Law was over one hundred pages long. I not only drew on legal authorities—statutes, decisions and citations—but also on sociological, criminological, literary, and philosophical sources. I was ready for a tough fight— and prepared for it.

# CHAPTER FOUR

The night before the trial I spoke to Rubenstein, Johnson and Allen. I asked them again whether they realized that a public trial and cross-examination could dig into their past, that there would be news coverage, and that their privacy would be sacrificed. In Johnson's case, his children would learn that their father had once been charged with a crime.

Each replied, as they had previously, that they were aware of the consequential sacrificial price of this fight.

Rubenstein simply stated: "Jean wants to take the witness stand." Johnson said: "Vi and I talked it over a long time and our position is still the same. I have made it. I owe to all the others who didn't make it to be in court and to do my best to fight for them." Allen said: "Will it be as bad as the South Pacific under fire?" I gained courage from Dave, Bill and his wife, James and his wife. Whatever fears I'd had, and there was much insecurity, disappeared. I was nervous (every lawyer is before trial), but I was now firmly determined to be my clients' equal in facing the next day's ordeal of uncertainty and the daunting consequences of defeat to the cause (and to me professionally and personally) should the powerful Police Department prevail.

In New York, cases ready for trial were assigned to a judge as soon as he completed a previous trial. This eliminated "jockeying" for partial or prejudiced judges. The case was referred to the late Judge Jacob Markowitz for trial.

I had never had any matter before Judge Markowitz and had not met him previously. I knew that he was a native New Yorker, raised on New York City's East Side. He was considered a good judge and, most important, was reputed to be a very humane and perceptive jurist.

In the early course of the trial I put Steve Allen on the witness stand as my first witness to accommodate his busy schedule of TV taping that day. He testified that Dave and James had appeared on his popular nationwide Sunday night TV program many times. There had never been any complaints from his many millions of viewers. On the contrary, the appearances of Dave and James had always resulted in a huge amount of mail expressing appreciation. Steve Allen testified that he would employ them again, and Bill too if he was available, with full knowledge of their past. He spoke highly of Dave's and James's characters and of their reputation in the world of music.

As Steve was testifying I observed Judge Markowitz looking intently over my shoulder at the public area of the court room. I glanced in that direction and was shocked to see Dave suffering agony. He was trembling, his face was wet, his teeth were chattering and his hands were pressed against his head. I knew that Dave was a wounded war veteran and had suffered from malaria as a result of his war experiences. I approached the bench and informed Judge Markowitz that Dave was one of the plaintiffs. The judge permitted me to interrupt my examination of Steve Allen and attend to Dave.

I escorted Dave from the court room and attempted to persuade him to go home with an escort. He wept and said that he could not leave the trial, that the attack would soon pass, that he should have brought the malaria medicine that Veteran's Administration hospital patients are required to have in their possession at all times in the event of an attack. He insisted that he would stay. He toppled over and I held him up. I promised him that he could testify the next day. He was escorted from the building. When I returned to the court room, it was procedurally advisable for me to state for the trial record Dave's unavailability as the plaintiff and request permission that he testify the next day regardless of the status of the trial due to his having suffered a malaria attack while waiting to testify.

As I spoke for the record, Judge Markowitz opened my memorandum of law which had been submitted before the trial and found the summary of Dave's life, career, and struggles. Judge Markowitz granted the request that Dave be permitted to testify the next day.

Dave's malaria attack in the court room added a new dimension to the trial—Dave, a plaintiff and an applicant for a Card, had suffered a war-consequent attack in full view of the judge and the public. Our plaintiffs and witnesses were no longer mere applicants before a Court, but human beings capable of suffering, agony, and tears. When Jean Rubenstein testified for Bill and spoke of his rehabilitation, his love for his child, and the emptiness of their home while he was on tour because he was not permitted to work in New York City, we were no longer concerned with abstract legalities but with the suffering of the wife. When James Johnson testified with impressive dignity, one was aware of him as a human being and gifted artist who expressed in his music the suffering of his people. When Bill Rubenstein testified, one felt compassion for this talented and attractive young man who was raised by a widowed mother and who was constantly reminded, possibly too often, of the high character and standards of his heroic father—a governmental official and war casualty.

Dave's malaria attack in court had added more valuable overtones to the trial than Steve Allen's persuasive testimony, my memorandum of law, or what his own testimony would have contributed had he sat in the witness chair.

When the Police Department officials testified, Judge Markowitz participated in the questioning and elicited the usual arrogant answers. Judge Markowitz asked Deputy Commissioner McElroy whether satisfactory proof of Bill's rehabilitation was not indicated by the fact that he had not been arrested in the last five years following his conviction of a misdemeanor, that he was married, had a family and was working to support them. The Deputy Commissioner replied that only a short time had elapsed since the last conviction.

Judge Markowitz repeated the question and added "How much more time is one to do to get work in New York?" "I'd expect another two years" answered Deputy Commissioner McElroy. I submit part of the Minutes and invite the reader to study the functioning of the bureaucratic mind.

THE COURT: With regard to Mr. Rubenstein, Commissioner, did you make a final decision before you had your minutes?

MR. RUDMAN [The City Attorney representing the Police Department]: He heard the testimony. He conducted the hearing. [Note: A falsehood fed the witness. Capt. O'Rourke conducted the hearing. The witness took his cue and contributed these two falsehoods.]

THE WITNESS: I conducted the hearing at that time, as I recollect, I called in a stenographer to have him read the transcript.

THE COURT: And you made notations?

THE WITNESS: That is right.

THE COURT: And you conducted the hearing?

THE WITNESS: That is right.

THE COURT: I insist on those minutes being presented before this trial is concluded. [Obviously, the Court detected the City Attorney's feeding the witness.]

Go ahead.

BY MR. RUDMAN:

Q Can you tell us why you turned down Mr. Rubenstein's application?

THE COURT: In 1958, sir.

A Because of his criminal record and character generally, and other factors.

Q What was his criminal record as you saw it in 1958?

A Well, as I recollect it, I think he was arrested four times in connection with narcotic drugs, of which he was convicted twice.

MR. COHEN: I move to strike it out, that the record of convictions speaks for itself.

The commissioner testified, "As I recollect." Let us not go on his recollection, sir.

THE COURT: Overruled.

A And also the fact that he admitted to being a producer or grower of marijuana; and in two instances, as I recollect it from the record, he was arrested in conjunction with a known seller of drugs.

MR. COHEN: If Your Honor please, I object to all that.

THE COURT: May I hear it? Let me hear the answer.

MR. COHEN: It is going into the record.

A And further, that this man had spent his life outside of New York City in other towns and developed this record in other places. He had not been previously employed in a cabaret in this city. There was a short period of time from—I think it was about less than two years—from the termination of his probation until his application for a card. There was not sufficient time elapsed in his own best interest, in my judgment, to permit him to enter as hazardous an area as employment in a cabaret is considered to be with respect to this type of crime. And I felt that a greater time should elapse for him to demonstrate, by exemplary conduct, that he had overcome these propensities for the commission of crime with respect to drugs, and such factors as that he was not being deprived of employment in this city that he never previously had.

MR. COHEN: I move to strike out that answer. The answer was concocted of "I recollect" and "I think." There was the actual record before the Commissioner and he was testifying on recollection.

Further, he was testifying, not as to the actual conviction of the man, but police reports in his possession which were never shown to Mr. Rubenstein, which we have never examined and which are absolutely hearsay.

It is fundamental, sir, in any administrative proceeding, that the private or confidential knowledge that the hearing officer may have cannot be used against a person applying for a particular license or privilege unless that person is accosted with the information, and Mr. Rubenstein was never shown this information, and I was never shown this information as his attorney.

The man is bound by a record of conviction and not by a record of police reports written by officers making reports. The Police Commissioner has been a patrolman and he knows the literary effort that goes into the writing of police records, the element of accuracy, the desire to impress a superior, and so forth.

No police officer, I contend, ever takes these reports seriously and the Commissioner is too much a man of integrity to have taken these reports on face value.

If the testimony is to be as to the convictions of Mr. Rubenstein, of course they should properly be in evidence and presented before the Court; but if the Commissioner is now rationalizing his position in denying the application by now making references to police records which were not in evidence at the first or second hearing, I think, Your Honor, that it is improper to encumber this record with that type of testimony.

\* \* \* \*

By Mr. Rudman:

Q   With respect to an application by J. J. Johnson—

The Court: Before you get to J. J. Johnson, I want to ask some questions on Mr. Rubenstein.

Mr. Rudman: I have no objection to Your Honor's asking him.

The Court: Commissioner, we are in 1958 now and not the 1957 matter.

Are you aware of the fact that Mr. Rubenstein was married?

The Witness: I was, yes.

The Court: And has a child?

The Witness: Yes, I was aware of that.

The Court: Does the stenographic record, if you recall, indicate whether or not there has been what I would characterize as "rehabilitation," and probably what you would characterize as "rehabilitation"?

The Witness: I don't know, Your Honor.

THE COURT: Am I to understand, sir, that Mr. Rubenstein, subsequent to the last conviction—which I believe was in 1954, is that right?

MR. RUDMAN: 1955. He was arrested in 1954 and convicted in 1955, and he was placed on probation which terminated in 1957.

THE COURT: Right. An act committed in 1954, sentenced in 1955, complying with probation, leading an exemplary life since that incident, and despite that fact, in your judgment, you felt he should not be issued a card?

THE WITNESS: That is right, Your Honor, considering the period of time, the years over which he had been committing these transgressions and the short lapse of time from the termination of his probation, I considered that sufficient time had not elapsed and at this time he should not be given a card.

THE COURT: Mr. Rubenstein was charged with the crime of the possession of marijuana?

THE WITNESS: Yes.

THE COURT: You don't consider that a serious felony, do you?

THE WITNESS: No, no, not in itself, no.

THE COURT: Does the age factor of one who might be indulging in the use of marijuana enter into the picture?

THE WITNESS: At the current—you mean at the time of the application?

THE COURT: If one is using it, and the fact that they are young and may have some problems and some company that they keep.

THE WITNESS: If he is using it at the time of the application I would hesitate to authorize his employment in a cabaret because of the circumstances attendant to such thing.

THE COURT: But if there was no proof that he was using it at the time of the application, or that he had used it for a number of years prior to the application—

THE WITNESS: Just for a user, two, three, years, for example—

THE COURT: You mean refraining from use for two or three years, in your opinion—

THE WITNESS: Yes, sir, considering other circumstances, his family, his liabilities and responsibilities, and reasonable—all we look for is a reasonable degree to believe that there is a rehabilitation.

THE COURT: And if one, in the course of using this in one's youth, may likewise have indulged in—what do you call it, raising it?

MR. RUDMAN: Growing it.

THE COURT: Growing it for his own use, and having refrained from growing it or using it for a number of years, what would your reaction be?

THE WITNESS: That, Your Honor, was an isolated instance.

THE COURT: What was an isolated instance?

THE WITNESS: One arrest, even, for growing it, and three or four years had elapsed. I would take that into consideration as probably being acceptable.

THE COURT: The last known act was in 1954, and he was placed on a year's probation with a suspended sentence in 1955, so we have at least three and a half years, if not four years.

THE WITNESS: Your Honor, I was taking one case.

THE COURT: I am taking the Rubenstein case.

THE WITNESS: I am taking the history of it, Your Honor. He was arrested four times over a period of years, showing a continuity of addiction to this practice, at least indicating that.

THE COURT: Now, Commissioner, let us take the record as you have it. In December 1951 he was arrested for a violation of 1752 Sub 1 of the Penal Law. Is that marijuana?

MR. COHEN: Yes, sir.

THE COURT: A user of marijuana. That was dismissed.

In January 1953 he was charged with a violation and given six months in the penitentiary and a fine, and it was paid, and he paid his debt to society.

In 1954 there was another charge, and that was dismissed.

In 1955, thereafter, there was a charge and he was placed on a year's probation. But since then there are no arrests or convictions. So we have a lapse of three and a half to four years since the last charge or act.

THE WITNESS: Yes.

THE COURT: And with a conceded state of facts, or not questioned if not conceded, that this man has married since and has a home and family, married to a young lady who certainly made a very presentable witness, formerly in the social service field, how much more is one to do to be able to work in New York?

THE WITNESS: I would expect at least another year to two years.

THE COURT: You do?

THE WITNESS: Yes, considering the entire record, Your Honor.

THE COURT: You do?

THE WITNESS: Yes.

THE COURT: Then you are going into a five or a six-year period for a youth who used marijuana and making that more severe than a serious felony.

THE WITNESS: Well, he was associated with producing it, and with a seller.

THE COURT: There is nothing in this record, sir, and I don't know what the minutes will show—

MR. RUDMAN: There is a report which the Commissioner considered from Syracuse, Onandaga, a full report, not from the social worker, his wife—

THE COURT: All of that precedes 1954. The Commissioner has testified in a serious felony, where a man has paid his debt, if he has been rehabilitated and a proper individual for five years, he certainly should have the right to a card.

MR. COHEN: May I interrupt, sir?

THE COURT: Just a moment, please.

That is what the Commissioner has indicated. Here we have a young man who, while at college and shortly thereafter, indulged in the use of marijuana. For the past three and a half to four years there is not a charge nor an arrest, nor a claim of any kind, nature or description, and we have every indication of rehabilitation, of good character, of wholesome work, and good family life. I think that is a fair statement in regard to the latter, Mr. Rudman, of what the record is.

MR. RUDMAN: There is this to be said, Judge. Mr. Rubenstein was 26 years old in 1955. He was no 17-year old youth.

THE COURT: Just a moment. Are you suggesting that a person of 25 who, five years ago, used marijuana, should be kept out forever?

MR. RUDMAN: No.

THE COURT: How long do you say, if his character is good and he leads a reasonable life?

MR. RUDMAN: I don't—

THE COURT: I will elect to find out from the Commissioner.

MR. RUDMAN: Another thing is this: Insofar as subsequent events are concerned, Mr. Rubenstein has been outside the City of New York, according to his wife's testimony, for at least 18 months, a good part of the year, and this record goes back to his fingerprint inquiry as of May 1957 or 1958, and there has been no new record obtained; isn't that so, Commissioner?

THE WITNESS: That is right.

MR. RUDMAN: What may turn up, I don't know.

THE COURT: Mr. Rudman, you are not going to get me to indulge in thinking that people are committing wrongs without proof and refuse them something that they otherwise might be entitled to. I don't buy that last thing—that you have no proof of any kind that he did anything wrong, but because you have no proof that that justifies it.

MR. RUDMAN: When he makes a new application—

THE COURT: He made an application in 1958.

MR. RUDMAN: That is correct.

THE COURT: I want to know why it was rejected.

BY MR. RUDMAN:

Q   What other convictions did he have, if you know?

A   Three convictions of operating without a license, license plates.

THE COURT: That was a determining factor?

THE WITNESS: Not a determining factor; it was considered.

Q None of these by itself was the determining factor?

A No.

THE COURT: Incidentally, all of those items preceded March 1954, likewise?

THE WITNESS: That is right.

THE COURT: So that, since March 1954, his record, as far as you know, is as wholesome and as fine as anybody's could be?

THE WITNESS: As far as I know.

THE COURT: And despite that fact you say he should be further rehabilitated?

THE WITNESS: Yes, because of the frequency of the offenses prior to that time.

BY MR. RUDMAN:

Q Did you take into consideration the fact that his probation expired in 1957?

A I did.

Q And also the fact that you had no evidence as to the time that elapsed after that?

A No. Our procedure is to consider following the term of probation.

THE COURT: How long after probation?

THE WITNESS: About a year and a half.

THE COURT: How long after a man has—

THE WITNESS: For the serious crimes, five years.

THE COURT: You recognize the use of marijuana is not in the same category you classify as a serious crime?

THE WITNESS: No, but the production of it is a serious thing.

THE COURT: He was not charged with any of that?

THE WITNESS: I know, but he admitted to it.

THE COURT: For his own use.

MR. RUDMAN: He didn't say that.

THE WITNESS: He didn't say that.

THE COURT: You have no proof that he sold it, have you, Commissioner?

THE WITNESS: No, no.

THE COURT: A man is still entitled to some inferences in his favor unless there is proof to the contrary.

BY MR. RUDMAN:

Q   If he had applied for a taxicab license, would you have given him a taxicab license?

A   No.

MR. COHEN: Objection.

THE COURT: Objection sustained.

MR. RUDMAN: I am just trying to show that this—

THE COURT: Objection sustained. Strike the answer. Off the record.

(Discussion off the record)

\* \* \* \*

THE COURT: Commissioner, pretty near a year has gone by since Mr. Rubenstein has made his application. Taking your calculation now, and with the proof in the case that he has been everything that one can desire, a normal human being, married and has a family, is there any reason today, now, forgetting what happened a year ago, that he should not get a card?

THE WITNESS: There is no reason that I know of that he cannot apply for a rehearing. What I will do about it, Your Honor, I will have to investigate so far as I can. But he has the right to apply for a rehearing, and I think counsel understands that; so does the applicant.

THE COURT: Do you want to ask just about Mr. Rubenstein, because Mr. Rudman was not finished. He was going into Mr. Johnson's matter, but I thought we would have continuity. So if you have questions, let it be just on Mr. Rubenstein.

REDIRECT EXAMINATION

BY MR. COHEN:

Q   Where does this sheet come from, Commissioner?

A   I don't know just at the moment.

Q   Where did you get it, sir?

THE COURT: It was part of the file.

A    It was part of the file.

MR. RUDMAN: It is in the Department records, transcripts made by the Department.

Q    Would you have the original disposition sheet in the file?

A    I don't know.

MR. RUDMAN: You have the Syracuse reports there.

Q    Commissioner, may I show you, while we are looking for that, the arrest of December 19th and January 9th?

1951, December 19th, 1951 arrested; January 9, 1952, charge dismissed; January 9, 1952, arrested; January 15, 1952, disposition. Are these considered by you as two arrests, Commissioner?

A    I don't know if that was the sheet I was looking at, or whether it was the record. I don't know if this sheet is the true copy of the arrest record or not.

Q    Commissioner, do you recollect in the testimony that Mr. Rubenstein testified that he had been arrested and the charge was technically dismissed, and then he was rearrested on another charge and this was one series of transactions, one arrest procedure, actually?

A    No, I don't recollect that.

MR. COHEN: I think you will find that in the minutes, sir. He was arrested on one charge and pleaded to another charge and technically rearrested. It is the same arrest. It happened twice. Actually, therefore, two arrests and not four arrests for the same offense.

THE COURT: Commissioner, from your experience in the Police Department, it is not unusual for a person to be charged or to be arrested and charged with one offense and immediately following a disposition of that matter, on the same state of facts, some other charge is made; is that right?

THE WITNESS: That is right.

THE COURT: Would you say, sir, bearing in mind these dates and bearing in mind the sections of law involved, December 19, 1951, violation 1752 Sub 1 of the Penal Law; January 9, 1952, dismissed. January 9, 1952, violation of Penal Law 1751 and 422, would you say that they arose out of the same chain of circumstances?

THE WITNESS: If that is a true copy, I would say yes, Your Honor. It indicates it there.

THE COURT: That is the same chain of circumstances, and there were not two arrests, but one arrest, and different charges. One of the charges was dismissed and on the other he was found guilty.

THE WITNESS: That could be, but I don't know if that is a true picture of the situation or not.

THE COURT: In the picture that I have before me that was handed to me by Mr. Rudman, the Corporation Counsel, as having come from the file that was before you with regard to this hearing; and likewise a similar or practically analogous situation of a violation on September 26, 1954, dismissed March 15, 1955, and on March 17th a violation of some other sections.

THE WITNESS: Well, there would be a two-day lapse there. That would not necessarily follow, Your Honor. There can be a general arrest on that one.

THE COURT: There might have been on the second one?

THE WITNESS: Yes.

THE COURT: But certainly as to the first one, your thinking is that in all likelihood it was all in one?

THE WITNESS: If that is correct. But I don't think the record really bears that out, Your Honor.

THE COURT: And you think that was of substantial materiality to defer giving Mr. Rubenstein in 1958, the right to work?

THE WITNESS: I considered it and took it into consideration, Your Honor, yes.

MR. COHEN: Plaintiffs' Exhibit 7 makes reference to arrest, but excepts traffic violations.

BY MR. COHEN:

Q   Is that correct, Commissioner?

A   I didn't get that, Mr. Cohen.

Q   Plaintiffs' Exhibit 7, which is the application form for a cabaret employee's identification card, I call your attention to provision No. 7 which asks if the applicant has had any arrests. Do you recollect the parenthetical statement which follows that?

A  Yes.

Q  What does it say?

A  Except traffic violations.

Q  There were three traffic violations on the Rubenstein matter, were there not?

A  There were.

Q  And traffic violations are specifically excluded on the application form?

A  On the application form, that's right.

Q  Nevertheless you took these traffic violations into consideration?

A  I certainly did, yes.

Q  Are traffic violations, Commissioner, a sign of moral turpitude?

The Commissioner glared! On cross-examination I questioned Deputy Commissioner McElroy. He stated in response to my question that he had reversed Inspector Lent and Captain O'Rourke's decisions because they did not conform to "standards." Whose? His. I thereupon sought to show that the Deputy Commissioner's standards reflected the totality of his strict religious beliefs and consequently would be subjective and arbitrary.

I drew the Judge's ire when I attempted to ask Deputy Commissioner McElroy: "Is it not a fact that you have two daughters who are nuns and two sons who are priests?" The question was struck from the record over my objections. (The Police Department thereafter portrayed me as anti-Catholic. I was later asked by one of my usually friendly police officials in a hurt tone of voice: "Why did you attack the Catholic Church in Court?" When I denied that I had attacked the Catholic Church in Court and related to him what had happened and the reasons for the question, he cautioned me that the word had been spread among the Catholic personnel in the Division that I had openly attacked Catholicism in the trial.)

Jackie Bright, National Secretary of the American Guild of Variety Artists, the only union official in the entertainment industry who had volunteered to testify, stated in response to cross-examination by the Police Department's attorney that in his opinion it would be more appropriate that the Police screen the night club customers rather than the night club entertainers and employees.

During the course of the trial, a judge may call all parties into Chambers for a conference and an informal off-the-record discussion can resolve problems. Judge Markowitz declared a recess and directed that we adjourn to his Chambers.

It is not considered proper for an attorney to discuss what is seen or heard in Chambers during or after a trial. The frank, often blunt, informality of off-the-record discussions is extremely valuable and is safeguarded by this unwritten gentleman's agreement. Suffice it to say that Rubenstein, Johnson, and Allen received their Cards. However, the issue of the Police Cards was not decided, ostensibly for technical reasons—"ostensibly"—but, from a realistic point of view, the Police Department's wall had now cracked and was crumbling.

I can now divulge that there was a "bargain" in chambers. In consideration of Cards to be issued to Rubenstein and Johnson (and other "benefits"), I withdrew the other causes of action without prejudice to my rights to institute other actions. The Police Department saved face—temporarily—but as far as the press and public were concerned, the Police Department had suffered a defeat.

In fact, soon thereafter the Mayor proposed that the Card system be moved from the Police Department to another agency. He was supported by the officials of the union in the industry in this suggestion. I vigorously opposed this apparent acknowledgment of victory on the grounds that, since it had been demonstrated that there was no explicit law authorizing the Cards, establishing the Card system in another agency would require passage of a law creating the

Card system. This shameful proposal was dropped. The Police still continued the unlawful Card system.

A few weeks later, I sent Judge Markowitz a three-column article about the trial published in Germany!

About a year later, I attended a court session which involved the Police Commissioner's attack on restaurant-cabaret establishments as a reprisal for what had happened to him at the Lord Buckley hearing to be discussed later in these pages. I was not involved, and I am sure that Judge Markowitz did not know that I was in the court room. In the course of the argument of the attorneys and the City's lawyers, he raised my memorandum of law on the Johnson, Rubenstein, and Allen case and stated that he had requisitioned the memorandum of law that morning from the files for use in the proceedings. "This memorandum was always correct . . . ," he stated.

# CHAPTER FIVE

I commenced another case with high hopes, but I had underestimated the Police Department. As the case was awaiting a decision, a drifter named Fred Thompson attacked and murdered a child. In the room where the child died, Thompson had left empty beer cans bearing his fingerprints. The room was thoroughly inspected on the Saturday when the child's body was discovered. The landlady of the boarding house and neighbors knew the identity and description of the room's occupant, Thompson.

Police procedure in homicide cases requires an immediate search for fingerprints to identify the perpetrator. Often the identity of the criminal can be established within an hour. Thompson's identity was known almost immediately.

However, the press was notified on Monday that on that day—i.e. two days later—Thompson had been identified because his fingerprints were on record on his Cabaret Employee Identification application. He had been a dishwasher many years previously. Although the Police Department facilities are open 24 hours a day every day of the year, the Department explained to the gullible press and public that they had to wait until Monday for their Division of Licenses to open so that they could examine the Cabaret Card records for fingerprints. Presumably, no one in the Police Department had the keys to the store and so they had to wait until Monday. (Thompson's fingerprints were on other records for previous crimes.)

The Hearst newspapers immediately blared that the case proved the value of the Cabaret Card system. The Hearst papers were joined by the usual sycophantic chorus of those eager to ingratiate themselves with the police. I quote a columnist from the *World-Telegram*:

> Supreme Court Justice Sidney A. Fine today upheld as "constitutional and valid" the Police Department regulation requiring identification cards for cabaret entertainers and employees. (It was a cabaret card which led to the identification of Fred J. Thompson, admitted killer of 4-year-old, Edith Kiecorius, who was captured this afternoon near Lakehurst, N.J.)

Notwithstanding this tawdry setback and what appeared to be a temporary "victory" for the Police Department, more cases followed, and the wall was cracking ever more rapidly. Sophie Tucker, Nina Simone, Dizzy Gillespie, Duke Ellington, Count Basie, and many other stars had Cards but would not exhibit them. The Rubenstein-Johnson decision had given employees the courage to defy the police.

Deputy Commissioner McElroy was removed, and a civilian was placed in charge of the Division. He was a Columbia Law School Professor, Leonard Reisman, a brilliant and sincere young man. We met in the course of two hearings in his Department and later during the Lord Buckley hearing. Professor Reisman did not last long in the Division; he was transferred to headquarters as a Deputy Commissioner in charge of Legal Affairs. (Later he helped to modernize the Police Academy. He accomplished wonders in this assignment. One day, unfortunately for the City, he suffered a fatal heart attack in the street.)

Although he was my adversary in the Police Card fight, I was certain that every aspect of that system was revolting to him as a liberal lawyer, a scholar, and an honorable and decent person. I regret that he once accused me of "patronizing" him. I attempted to assure him that this was not so. What he regarded as "patronizing" was a reluctance on my part to hit him as hard as I had his predecessors, because—this may seem incredible—Leonard Reisman bore an unusual physical resemblance to my younger brother, Bernard. He looked more like my brother than I did; indeed, they could have passed for twins.

Professor Reisman was succeeded by another civilian, a former F.B.I. agent, Edward J. McCabe. Mr. McCabe was exceedingly fair but was still part of the system. He, too, soon left the Division.

I instituted several other cases thereafter. The American Civil Liberties Union and a number of distinguished individuals and performers were now openly expressing their disapproval of the system.

Billie Holiday is for some illogical reason identified with the Police Card Cases. However, she refused to become involved in spite of the urgings of her friends and associates. I spent hours trying to persuade her lawyers to ask her to join my plaintiffs in test cases—at no charge or expense to her. She refused—and, lo and behold, posthumously gained fame as a liberal fighter for civil rights and in opposing the Police Cards. Not one of the so-called militant artists became involved or volunteered to join in the test cases, even at no cost. For most of them, it was easier to verbalize hatred and bigotry than to assume a sense of relationship to fellow artists or employees.

Not a single union official in the entertainment industry, with the exception of Jackie Bright of AGVA, assisted me or sought independently to fight the Police Card cases at that time. Under pressure from their membership, however, union officials were beginning to grumble slightly about the Card system.

The challenge to the Police Department was now becoming progressively more daring. Many more musicians and performers were refusing to apply for Police Cards, and, if they had Cards, they refused to show them to their employers. Some of these employers refused to ask their employees for Cards and declined to enter the Card-holding employee's name and card number as required in their Employment Record books.

The police were conspicuously challenged by formerly cringing cabaret and hotel employees and employers. They responded in the only way possible—constant inspections, summonses, threats, and suspensions. These reprisals now opened up another battle front for me—hearings for employers, with the press present.

Two employers who had courageously fought the Police Department on the Police Card issue became the prime targets. These two employers, the Den and the Village Gate, were not beholden to the Mafia, gangsters, politicians or any criminal element. Individuals owned these restaurant-cabarets, and they had invested their own funds.

The police visited the Den and the Village Gate at irregular times and disturbed the operations by constant inspections and freely issued summonses and violations to the two restaurants. In one instance, the police engaged in an activity which could have become a disaster for the Den.

One afternoon I received a phone call from Eddie Leipzig, manager of the Den and the owner's son. "Two detectives are here," he told me. I asked, "Are the various licenses and permits conspicuously displayed?" (This was the usual offense which resulted in the issuance of a summons. Since over thirty licenses and permits were required to be displayed on the walls of the small cubbyhole offices, those licenses which could not be displayed for lack of room were placed on top of the desk in the office. Consequently, the Police Department Inspector could always determine that the permits were not "conspicuously displayed" and thus violated Police Department rules and regulations. The summons would require appearance at a hearing. Violations could result in suspension, usually over a weekend, the busiest time for the restaurant-cabaret, or loss of a license.)

Eddie replied, "They didn't look for licenses. They're in the back, where the dressing rooms are." I shouted to a startled Eddie: "Get off the phone and stay with them! Watch everything they do!" But he said, "They just passed me. They're leaving." I told Eddie to go with one of the porters into the dressing room and inspect every inch of the room—to open make-up jars, insert a pencil into coldcream and cosmetic jars and examine the pockets of all dressing gowns and suits and to look for planted narcotics, weapons, or inflammable materials.

Eddie phoned me within a quarter of an hour. "We found an envelope with white powder in Lenny Bruce's room under a towel." I told him to flush it down the toilet immediately and call the local Precinct, with whom the Leipzigs were friendly. "Ask them if the two detectives came out of that Precinct. If so, get their names and call me back." Eddie called his friend who commanded the Precinct and then reported to me that "the Captain says they are not his detectives. He thinks they are headquarters men and said, 'If the bastards show up later, get their names; don't let them in and call me back, either at the Precinct or at home.' He thinks we're being set up for a raid." I told Eddie: "Don't let any cops or detectives in tonight on the cuff. If you know the cops, explain to them that you are being inspected and, in order to protect yourself and them, you don't want them in the place."

Two detectives showed up that night. Eddie demanded their names, but they left at once without giving them. One of the employees told me that Eddie exploded in anger at the attempted frame-up and then called the Precinct in their presence. In any event, from that time on Eddie would not permit any inspection until every available employee was present in the room with the inspecting officers.

The Village Gate was a prime target. The owners were brothers. Art D'Lugoff has a Master's degree in Political Science from New York University and is a graduate of Yeshiva University. Bert D'Lugoff is a physician who at the time also taught at Johns Hopkins University Medical School. Obviously, they were two unusual club owners.

One night two detectives showed up during a performance. They began to issue a summons for "poor lighting." Since the stage was illuminated during the performance, the rest of the club was, of course, in diminished light, but certainly not dark. Art ran down the aisle shouting, "Stop the show." He stepped on the stage and told the audience of some 400 patrons that the police were harassing him because of his fight against the Police Cards and that two detectives were issuing him a summons because of poor lights. "Is there any darkness here?" Art asked his customers. "No," roared the customers. "Will you be my witnesses?" "Yes," everyone shouted. "Good. The waiters will take your names and addresses and I will notify you of the hearing."

The detectives now added another complaint to the summons: "Inciting a riot and endangering the safety of two detectives."

At the hearing before the newly appointed Deputy Commissioner Reisman, Art appeared with his witnesses, actor Theodore Bikel and Lorraine Hansberry, author of *Raisin in the Sun,* as well as a number of newspaper reporters who had been at the Village Gate on the eventful evening, and a few employees.

I introduced the list of names of the 400 witnesses and asked that Bikel's and Hansberry's testimony be deemed what the absent witnesses would have testified were they present at the hearing. This can be done to avoid repetitious or cumulative testimony on the same issue. The motion was granted. I then asked Deputy Commissioner Reisman, since two detectives were involved and only one had appeared at the hearing, that the testimony of the second detective be required, both as a corroborating witness and because the complaint stated that the safety of two detectives was endangered.

The Deputy Commissioner stated that he could not obtain the testimony of the second detective at that time. No reason was given. I knew the reason: "Commissioner," I said,

> Since the second detective was sentenced to a five-year prison term yesterday, we can either adjourn this hearing for five years without prejudice, or subpoena

the detective from prison to testify, or I can move to dismiss the complaint because there is no proof that there was a riot, nor was there any incitement to riot. Further, there is no proof that the two detectives' safety was in danger, and finally, because the weight of the testimony is proof that there was no violation of the adequate lighting requirement.

Deputy Commissioner Reisman dismissed the proceedings.

Lorraine told me, "Max, if I wrote this in a play, no one would believe it."

To ease the situation, I introduced Commissioner Reisman to Lorraine, to Bikel, and to the reporters.

The acknowledgments were reserved on both sides, however.

# CHAPTER SIX

The telephone caller introduced himself as "Doc Humes," so I deferentially replied, "Yes, doctor?" The caller said, "I am not a doctor. Doc is my nickname. I am a novelist and writer. I am calling you at the suggestion of Dorothy Schiff, publisher of the *New York Post.*" I told Humes that Mrs. Schiff and I did not know each other. He assured me that Mrs. Schiff knew me, or of me, because the *Post* had written about me and the Police Card cases and hearings. Humes wanted to see me on behalf of his friend, Lord Buckley. I told Humes that I did not know the gentleman, but we made an appointment to meet.

Harold Humes was then about 35 years old, the author of two well-received novels and one of the founders and editors of *The Paris Review.* His friend Lord Buckley was in his fifties and was a monologist. His given name was Richard but he always referred to himself, and was professionally known, as Lord Buckley.

Buckley had recently come to New York from Chicago to appear in cabarets and on TV. He had been employed in a cabaret when the police compelled the owner to dismiss him immediately because he had failed to indicate in his application for a Police Card that he had been convicted about 18 years previously in Reno on a drunk charge and had been arrested almost 19 years previously on a marijuana charge which was subsequently dropped. He had never been arrested since.

Humes accompanied Buckley to the Police Department to retrieve his Card so that he could resume his employment. Since there had been no hearing when Buckley's Card was lifted, Humes had assumed that a conference would result in its restoration.

Humes had hoped to record an attempt by a Police Department employee to solicit a bribe. He had a recorder hidden in his sleeve. No bribe was solicited. Humes asked me whether I wanted to hear the tape. I told him that I had no interest in the taped interview, assuming erroneously that the tape contained the familiar interview and denial. Nevertheless Humes sent me a transcript of the tape. I listened and was shocked.

Lord Buckley had no funds. Would I accept the case? I was told that Buckley's reputation was good. He was married, had appeared overseas more than a dozen times with the U.S.O. to entertain troops, and had appeared many times on the Ed Sullivan TV show. I told Humes that I would accept the case without fee.

I arranged a hearing for November 3, 1960, before Inspector Lent. I did not foresee any difficulty and expected that Inspector Lent would accept Buckley's explanation that he had failed to mention the arrest almost two decades before because he had forgotten it. I told Lord Buckley and Humes that I would need only one or two character witnesses.

Unfortunately, the exuberant Humes invited over thirty witnesses, including novelist Norman Mailer and a number of other well-known writers and newspaper reporters.

Inspector Lent was annoyed, and so was I. I knew that the presence of a number of newspaper reporters at a simple hearing would antagonize Lent.

It was then that I learned for the first time that Lord Buckley had a great number of admirers among authors, editors, and publishers because of his unique use of hip language as well as his fey personality. I had never heard Lord Buckley perform, but I had once listened to a radio broadcast of one of his records. It was fascinating.

Lord Buckley's hearing commenced rather awkwardly. The usual hearing before Inspector Lent was in his small office. Because of the number of witnesses, it was necessary to use the hearing room, thereby wasting an hour.

I argued the familiar objections: that the Police Department had no jurisdiction, that an inquiry as to an arrest so many years earlier was highly improper, and that the Police Department regulations themselves did not permit the Division to revoke or suspend temporary Cards until the card holder had received a "Notice and Hearing."

Lord Buckley testified well. Towards the end of his testimony he stated, completely unconscious of the irony of his remarks, that after his Card had been lifted he had been invited to appear as a performer, gratis, at the dinner of the Police Department's most prestigious organization, the Honor Legion. I had not been informed of this.

In some surprise, I began to ask Lord Buckley why the Honor Legion had invited him, but he interrupted in anticipation of an entirely different question. "Because I love the fuzz. I love all men."

The prosecuting police officer, now hard pressed to justify what was most obviously an unwarranted revocation of Lord Buckley's Card, pointed out that about four years earlier Lord Buckley had several traffic offenses in California. Inspector Lent, somewhat annoyed, crisply told the prosecuting police officer that the application explicitly exempted traffic offenses.

Inspector Lent made some barely audible comments about the late hour and the number of witnesses at hand and adjourned the hearing.

On November 7, 1960, I was notified that the hearing had been "re-set for 10 A.M., Monday, Nov. 14, 1960." Since the Card had been lifted without notice or hearing on October 19, 1960, this meant that Lord Buckley would be condemned to three weeks of unemployment. The adjournment would have a fatal consequence and climax that no one could foresee.

In retrospect, I am certain that Inspector Lent would have awarded Lord Buckley his Card that very day, had we started on time, had so many literary and press character witnesses not appeared, and had the hour not been so late. Ironically, I had planned to call only one character witness to testify.

My wife and I invited Lord Buckley to be our guest at Elsa Lanchester's concert. He told us why he referred to himself as "Lord" and why he granted to his many friends such titles as "Prince," "Earl," "Duke," and "Lady"—because "there is nobility in every person, and I acknowledge this." He was serious. There was a curious naïveté and charm about him. We were introduced to Elsa Lanchester. She had heard of Lord Buckley and was evidently pleased that he praised her performance. (We were relieved: How does one introduce a "Lord" Buckley to a British national?)

We discussed the hearing scheduled for later. We were optimistic. Lord Buckley was eager to return to work.

Lord Buckley died on Saturday, November 12, of malnutrition and alleged kidney trouble. He had been too proud to tell his friends that he was penniless and that he had no food.

His death set in immediate motion an amazing series of events. Indeed, Lord Buckley's passing tolled the bell for the now inevitable destruction of the Police Card system. His funeral coincided with the beginning of the end of the Police Commissioner, who was the embodiment and personification of unlimited police power.

The day after Lord Buckley died, I reread the transcript of the tape referred to by Doc Humes. I was stunned by what the tape portrayed. Political scientists, civil rights workers, and music and stage devotees will find the transcript invaluable. The tape must also be read as the prelude to the extraordinary confrontation with the police two days after Lord Buckley's death by over seventy of America's leading writers, editors, and publishers.

The tape, as noted above, was recorded by Humes when he and Lord Buckley had appeared before Sgt. Z, who was one of the officials in charge of the Police Card Division. Sgt. Z denied the request.

Sgt. Z had obtained a law degree while on the force; he

was a career man and seemed likely to go far in the Department; he was married and had a large family; he looked younger than his years. Unfortunately, he had become an automaton; the lawyer and family man had become absorbed by and into the system. The tape transcript was an exhibition of insensitive arrogance and official narrowness completely contrary to Sgt. Z's true character. A lawyer and family man can be programmed by an official system so that his qualities of equity, compassion, and generosity can be blunted, just as a young and otherwise warm man can be mechanized at times to bomb women and children in the heat of war.

If Buckley was a victim—so was Sgt. Z.

I submit a portion of the tape transcript as a clinical study of typical bureaucratic reasoning and speech. ("Z" is the sergeant; "B" is Buckley; "H" is Humes.)

Z: Were you ever arrested?

B: It was so many years ago. Was it some small arrest of some kind?

Z: You don't know?

B: Well, I don't recall.

Z: You don't recall 1941, 1943, 1944, 1946?

B: Was it for drinking?

Z: One was 1941 . . . That one was for drinkin'.

H: How long will it be before he can get his Card back?

Z: At such time as there's a hearing.

H: Why don't you have the hearing first and pull the Card later?

Z: If you had told the truth we would have.

B: Yeah, I was wrong, I guess.

H: Would you have given him a Card?

Z: Not if he admitted everything (unintelligible).

H: It's your jurisdiction to decide this?

Z: Yeah.

H: I'm a friend of Lord Buckley's, and I was just curious to know why people come around and pick up his Card without giving him any reason.

Z: Well, he's well aware of his criminal record.

H: These are criminal charges (unintelligible) . . .

Z: Using reefers, marijuana and tax act.

H: Are there any convictions on these?

B: There were no convictions.

Z: There's no conviction on that . . . This we got to ascertain yet.

H: But you pull the Card first and ascertain that afterwards. Is that right? Is there a statute that authorizes you to do this?

Z: That's right . . . Administrative Code of the City 436-1.

H: That you can lift somebody's cabaret Card?

Z: Uh-huh . . .

H: This is all new to me, and I'm anxious to know why.

B: How long will it be before we can get a hearing?

Z: Whenever you file a request for it, then you'll have one.

B: Do you have the hearing here?

Z: Upstairs.

H: How long will it be? He's not able to work without that Card, according to you.

Z: That's right.

H: What happens if he works without the Card?

Z: Then we give the premises a violation and we close them.

H: You close down the premises? Pretty rough way to treat people, don't you think?

Z: It depends on the people.

H: Depriving a man of his livelihood without due process of law?

Z: There are some people when they're selling narcotics say we're depriving them of their livelihood (unintelligible).

H: This is a different thing; he's an entertainer.

Z: It's not a different thing.

H: You don't lift a taxi-driver's license before you . . .

Z: We'd lift it more quicker than we would ever lift an entertainer's.

H: How many years ago was this?

Z: The last one, the (unintelligible) tax act was 1946.

The 1956 is minor. Six traffic misdemeanors—
whatever they are.

H: Well those aren't criminal; I mean, a traffic offense
is not criminal, when you speak of a criminal
record. Are there any convictions on these?

Z: This is what we are sending to find out—to ascertain.

B: What shall we do? Call you back on it?

Z: We asked him the question, "Were you ever
arrested?"

B: I said "No," because (unintelligible).

Z: We are lifting it on the false statement on the
application.

H: I see. But you also state that if he had said that he
was arrested, even if there were no convictions, you
wouldn't have given him a Card?

Z: If he would have proved there was no conviction at
that time, then there would have been (unintelligible) question to be determined, depending on
(unintelligible).

H: Would you know a way he can have his Card while
this is being ascertained?

Z: No.

H: Why is that? Is there any point to that? I'm just
trying to understand why he can't work. He needs
the money very badly.

Z: He may need the money very badly, but his
involvement as far as reefers and marijuana . . .

H: But there was no conviction on that! Now, in fact
there was a nol-prossed, is that right?

Z: Has he got proof of that to show us at this time?

H: Well, I mean the point is, don't you need some
stronger evidence than that?

Z: No we don't. The evidence that I'm going on, I'm
basing on his false statement. From there I'm going
to investigate.

H: The traffic offenses—do you have to put them
down, too, with the rest of them?

Z: Not the traffic offenses. Other than traffic.

H: But my point is: What about double jeopardy? It

seems to me that when he was arrested, there was no conviction.

Z: This has been tested in the courts and you want to test it again. If you want to test it, you can.

H: What tests in the court? Can you give me decisions on that?

B: If I have proof there was no conviction, can I get a Card?

H: How long will it take to get a hearing? You see, I have a percentage of this man's livelihood, and I'm very profoundly concerned about that, because it's going to jeopardize his. . . . He's just booked into the city for the first time, and we have other dates lined up for him, and this is very seriously liable to jeopardize him. If there's a false arrest here, it seems to me the city is liable for it.

Z: There is no false arrest here.

H: But you are certain that you can pull a man's Card, and this has been tested in the courts?

Z: That's right.

H: Can you give me the decision on them?

Z: Friedman vs. Valentine—the year, that's about '46. If you look up the administrative code . . .

H: This is all new to me, and I couldn't get hold of an attorney to come with us on this.

Z: You will find there have been numerous citations under it.

B: Do you know how soon the hearing will be?

Z: Well, I'll tell you. You want to request a hearing now. Is that correct?

H: As soon as possible. Is it possible to have the hearing this afternoon and clear this up?

B: Couldn't a phone call clear this up? Or I could call the attorney who defended me on it in Washington. If the attorney calls him or writes him . . .

Z: At the hearing, we'll inquire into the circumstances of these arrests and you'll explain them.

H: When will the hearing be?

Z: Well, that's what I'm asking you. Whenever you

request it. Either Tuesday, Wednesday, or Thursday in the afternoon.

H: Why can't you have it tomorrow? You mean he's going to be out of work this entire week, which probably means the end of his contract?

Z: Could be.

H: Could be? And it doesn't concern you any more than that. . .? Not when its. . .? Who put this power in your hands? That's what I can't understand. Who put this power in your hands?

Z: People (unintelligible).

H: Let me jot down a number of the statute.

Z: 434 of the charter and 436 . . . It's the administrative code and a charter of the city. 434 of the charter and 436 of the administrative code, and the key case is the city vs. . . Friedman vs. Valentine.

B: Tuesday, Wednesday and Thursday. Let's see. Can you ascertain by Tuesday whether there is no conviction on the case?

Z: We'll attempt to, yes.

H: This is liable to jeopardize his entire future livelihood.

Z: Could be.

H: Could be! My God! Suppose someone did this to you.

Z: We have the attitude we would like to keep a certain type of element out of this field. That's our purpose.

H: When you say "a certain type of element," you make a statement which is prejudicial to . . . I mean . . . There is no conviction on this.

Z: Well, this I don't know. That's what we have to find out. If I say his statement wasn't false on here and he admitted it and I was dismissed then I would . . .

B: . . . I was excited . . .

H: If I hadn't had a conviction, then I would probably put down "No" because he's already said (unintelligible).

Z: The question is, "were you ever arrested?"

H: I don't see what you're driving at. My point is that

if you make a statement, if you admit this, you won't give a Card. The man's livelihood is at stake.

Z: It depends on (unintelligible). If he admits he wasn't convicted, and admits that he was using narcotics . . .

H: Well, I don't think there is any statement that you can adduce from this thing alone.

Z: No. I'm just saying just as an example, under certain circumstances . . .

H: (to Buckley): Is this the case you told me about 15 years ago?

B: Yeah.

H: (to Sergeant again): Can I call you back on it . . .? What is your name?

Z: Sgt. Z.

H: What are these? Are these traffic?

Z: No. One was disorderly conduct in Nevada.

H: Misdemeanor?

Z: I assume that it may even only be an offense. I don't know. In Indianapolis, it was vagrancy.

H: That's also a misdemeanor. Is that right?

Z: No. Well, that's an offense, but that was dismissed. If it wasn't, I would have referred you to the State Liquor Authority, because I didn't have the power to give you a license. Since that would be (unintelligible).

H: No power to give a Card?

Z: Yeah.

H: You mean a vagrancy charge is a record?

Z: Depending on . . . You have to ascertain what the vagrancy was, because all types of procuring is vagrancy.

H: This is astonishing to me. This gives us the power of censorship . . .

Z: Procuring is vagrancy. Every type of prostitution is vagrancy.

H: Well, if you're charged with prostitution, it's not vagrancy?

Z: (unintelligible).

H: Not under the law . . .

Z: Under the law, mister. You're talking like you don't know what you're speaking of.

H: You mean that a vagrancy charge, if someone's up for vagrancy, and it's dismissed, you can keep the Card?

Z: If somebody was up for prostitution, he's charged with vagrancy. That's the charge. The technical charge. There is no charge prostitution.

H: Well, it's procuring, isn't it?

Z: Yeah, and it's also under the vagrancy section. You see, that's the problem (unintelligible).

B: We better call you back and get a hearing on it.

Z: Another thing is, you want to pick the time for the hearing. It has to be Tuesday, Wednesday, or Thursday afternoon.

H: That means he's out of work for a week.

B: Possibly he can't help it.

H: Yeah, but this means the end of his contract, too. There's no way you can let him work this week and then do this thing?

Z: Not in this space of time.

H: Does it say this is the statute, that you must lift the Card before this . . .

Z: It don't say this, no. It's understood policy.

H: That's a policy which you people make?

Z: That's right.

H: Who do they go to about seeing this policy changed? I would like to have him working this week, if possible.

Z: I'm the one in charge here now and I . . .

H: It doesn't do any good to prevent the man from earning a livelihood.

Z: Well.

B: I guess it's a question of the rules.

H: Well, I'm just questioning these rules.

Z: Well, you're not alone in questioning.

H: If the statutory authority for this case is one thing, but if this is a policy I would like to press for an allowance. I would like to ask for a waiver since the charge was dismissed.

Z: That we wouldn't give on one that turns in the F.B.I. (unintelligible).

B: They don't know whether there's a conviction on it. That's the hangup. There was no conviction. It was nol-prossed.

H: But I mean, a man is innocent until proved guilty in this country.

Z: No . . .

H: It seems to me that you're depriving him of a livelihood and also you're seriously jeopardizing his future. It's his first time in New York.

Z: Uh-huh.

H: And we've got club dates lined up for him.

Z: There are many fields that if you made a false statement on the application, they would also deny you employoment. Right?

H: I don't see where you have any business asking him in the first place, to tell you the truth.

Z: You can take that up with the legislature.

B: We'll call you back.

H: Thank you.


The scene was the dismal squad room of the Police Department Division of Licenses, in a converted warehouse near the Hudson River. The participating cast comprised Buckley, the unrealistic dreamer, shown here floating helplessly in the muddled stream of official attitudes and language; Humes, the sophisticated and internationally recognized welder of words and ideas, spluttering inarticulately when confronted with official and intransigent speech; and Sergeant Z, basically a decent man, but here the ventriloquist's dummy of the Department, mouthing self-righteous speech patterns with repetitious obstinacy.

Did Sgt. Z's attitude, comments, replies, and retorts result in a singular and unique experience, unlike that of any other Police Authority? Let us revert to Judge Markowitz's courtroom and the testimony of Deputy Police Commissioner McElroy. The Commissioner was a career man: an honest and decent man; four of his children had devoted their lives to service to their church as priests and nuns. One of the principal tenets of his religion and church—in fact all religions—was redemption, forgiveness, assistance to the fallen and unfortunate, the Golden Rule.

THE COURT: And with a conceded state of facts, or not questioned if not conceded, that this man has married since and has a home and family, married to a young lady who certainly made a very presentable witness, formerly in the social service field, how much more is one to do to be able to work in New York?

THE WITNESS: I would expect at least another year to two years.

THE COURT: You do?

THE WITNESS: Yes, considering the entire record, Your Honor.

THE COURT: You do?

THE WITNESS: Yes.

THE COURT: Then you are going into a five or a six-year period for a youth who used marijuana and making that more severe than a serious felony.

\* \* \* \*

MR. RUDMAN: Another thing is this: Insofar as subsequent events are concerned, Mr. Rubenstein has been outside the City of New York, according to his wife's testimony, for at least 18 months, a good part of the year, and this record goes back to his fingerprint inquiry as of May 1957 or 1958, and there has been no new record obtained; isn't that so, Commissioner?

THE WITNESS: That is right.

MR. RUDMAN: What may turn up, I don't know.

THE COURT: Mr. Rudman, you are not going to get me to indulge in thinking that people are committing wrongs without proof and refuse them something that they otherwise might be entitled to. I don't buy that last thing—that you have no proof of any kind that he did anything wrong, but because you have no proof that that justifies it.

MR. RUDMAN: When he makes a new application—

THE COURT: He made an application in 1958.

MR. RUDMAN: That is correct.

THE COURT: I want to know why it was rejected. . . .

THE COURT: So that, since March 1954, his record, as far as you know, is as wholesome and as fine as anybody's could be?

THE WITNESS: As far as I know.

THE COURT: And despite the fact you say he should be further rehabilitated?

THE WITNESS: Yes, because of the frequency of the offenses prior to that time.

# CHAPTER SEVEN

Had Lord Buckley been granted the required notice and hearing before his Card was lifted; had his Card been restored to him by Sgt. Z, the system-man; had he been permitted to work in New York, notwithstanding an arrest almost two decades previously, he would have earned the means to support his wife and two young children then residing in Nevada, and he would have had the funds to buy food to sustain his life. Lord Buckley died as cruelly and as forlornly as the One whose message he had transmitted in hip language to cabaret audiences: ". . .It is a better deal to treat the cat or his chick as you would like him to treat you. . . ."

I am sure that this was Lord Buckley's prayer as he died: "Big Daddy, give the fuzz their working card as humans . . . Big Daddy, give the fuzz a break for they know not what they do . . . I am hungry, Big Daddy, ain't had no food for two days . . . Man, it hurts. Peace for the fuzz. Peace for the cats. Peace for the chicks. . . . Big Daddy, it pains no more. . ."

Lord Buckley died on Saturday night, November 12, 1960. Within twenty-four hours, the early editions of Monday's *Herald-Tribune, New York Times, Daily News, and Daily Mirror,* available Sunday night, published on their front pages the extraordinary news of a meeting Sunday afternoon of a Citizens' Emergency Committee, comprising more than seventy of the City's most distinguished writers, editors, publishers, composers, and other public figures, at George Plimpton's apartment in the East Seventies. Most of them knew Lord Buckley. All those present were determined to fight the Police Department Cabaret Card system. All

present believed that the Police Department bore the moral
guilt for Lord Buckley's death.

The gathering was amazing. Never before in the history of
the City of New York or the United States had so many
literary figures and celebrities gathered on such short notice
to fight not for themselves but for others—porters, waiters,
chefs, bartenders, musicians, performers, and rehabilitated
former offenders.

The names of those present on the Citizens' Emergency
Committee should be recorded as an Honor Roll. Unfortunately, I have no record of all their names in my available
files. However, from the news accounts I learned that the
following, among others, comprised some of the founders
and members of the Citizens' Emergency Committee: novel-
ist Norman Mailer, editor Norman Podhoretz, writers Midge
Decter, Barney Rossett of Grove Press, Harold Humes, Nat
Hentoff, George Plimpton, Ring Lardner, Jr., Gilbert
Milstein of the *New York Times,* producer Lewis Allen,
writer Donald Ogden Stewart, composer David Amram,
Elaine Lorillard (a founder of the Newport Jazz Festival),
Random House editor Jason Epstein, Art D'Lugoff, Dr.
Bert D'Lugoff, performer Orson Bean, writer Lloyd Mc K.
Garrison, sociologist Dr. Charles Winick, financier Henry
D. Sedgwick, playwright Jack Geller, editor John Appleton,
record producer Al Ham, editor Robert Silver, actor Theo-
dore Bikel, playwright Lorraine Hansberry, publisher and
producer Robert Nemirov, singer Nina Simone, musicians
Quincy Jones, Johnny Richards, Eddie Duchin, Jr., Dizzy
Gillespie and Stan Getz, and also Peggy Hitchcock, niece of
my law school classmate, the late Frank Hitchcock. Also
participating in the Committee, a number of newspaper
reporters asked not to be recorded because of their employ-
ments; the editors of *Down Beat* magazine; Alan Morrison of
*Ebony* and *Jet* magazines and some of the editors and writers
from these publications; music critics Dan Morgenstern,
Stanley Dance, George Hoefer, Don Gold, Dom Cerulli,
Leonard Feather, Charles Suber, John Tynan, Ira Gitler;

Leo Shull, editor and publisher of *Show Business;* and many others. In addition to the Committee, there were many other public well-wishers—columnists Bob Sylvester, Jesse H. Walker, Earl Wilson, Ed Sullivan; civil liberties lawyers Stephen and Judith Vladick, the staff of *Variety,* and *New York Post* writers Bill Dufty, William H. A. Carr; some of the eighty members of the American Guild of Variety Artists who held a meeting and petitioned their organizations to participate in the fight; and a great number of other musicians and performers.

That night, the press published Ed Sullivan's tribute to Lord Buckley: "He was a wonderful, decent man. During the war he was part of my troupe that entertained in hospitals all over the country. Nobody found it necessary to screen him then or have him carry a police card."

Lord Buckley's family and friends were strong in their determination that I appear at the hearing adjourned to November 14 to obtain the card for Lord Buckley posthumously. They believed that Lord Buckley, who had entertained millions for over forty years and who had patriotically performed for troops and for casualties in hospitals hundreds of times, deserved at least the recognition that he was a worthy citizen of good repute.

The family was not vindictive and did not condemn the Police Department for the death of their husband and father—"Lord Buckley would not wish to have malice or revenge in our hearts," said Mrs. Buckley.

I told the Citizens' Emergency Committee that I would appear at the hearing. I asked that there be no demonstrations or large attendance at the hearing. I expressed the opinion that Inspector Lent would sensitively appreciate the situation and would grant the Card posthumously, but that any large attendance would create tensions. My request was debated, and finally it was decided that there would be three character witnesses available to testify: Ed Sullivan, Harold Humes, and Harry Sedgwick. If Sullivan were needed, Humes would phone him.

The press announced that the family had requested the hearing. I did not foresee any problem and expected to return to my office in time for an eleven o'clock appointment.

On Monday, November 14, I appeared at the Division of Licenses with Harry Sedgwick. I saw the Police Commissioner, a number of police officials, TV cameramen, photographers, and reporters. I told Sedgwick that there must be some important matter to attract this gathering, but that we would be out within one hour, since most of the Lord Buckley testimony had been taken at the first hearing.

The first knowledge I had that my surmise was wrong was when Inspector Lent told me, in a somewhat apologetic voice, that all were present for the Lord Buckley hearing. The Police Commissioner had directed his top staff to attend and requested the media to be present. He was going to show the Citizens' Emergency Committee; yes sir, good old Haman was going to hang this aggregation of intellectual and socially reformist Mordecais who dared to criticize the Police Department.

I was taken aback. I had not anticipated anything but a routine concluding hearing before a decent official, with only one or two witnesses.

We were directed to a large hearing room. I sat in front with Harry Sedgwick. Facing us were Police Commissioner Kennedy, Inspector Lent, Deputy Commissioner Reisman, and a number of other officials, some seated, some standing behind the Commissioner. At the side of the room were TV and press cameramen and reporters. (The *Daily News* reported that the number of top brass, a detective taking shorthand, a patrolman with a tape recorder, "badly outnumbered" the reporters present. However, during the course of that eventful day, the officials slipped out, and more reporters and TV personnel showed up as news of the activity at the hearing spread.)

The Police Commissioner sat about six feet in front of me. This was the first time we had seen each other face to face.

He was grim and tense, chain-smoking. His lips were tight and cruel. His jaw was thrust forward. His eyes glittered venomously. He conveyed the impression of a repressed volcano.

Our eyes met. I saw in him the horrors of my childhood in East Harlem (most of them discussed in my book *Autobiographical Essay: Youth in East Harlem*): the principal of P.S. 83, the martinet Captain Regis, the bigoted Mrs. Fippinger, the righteous church workers who did not see physically present black workers, the disciplinarian at the high school, the callous teachers whom I escaped by playing hookey and becoming a school dropout. All the hated, insensitive authorities were embodied in that man sitting in front of me.

I am usually a controlled person, especially at trials, hearings, and conferences. I would have been controlled at this hearing, but for the fact that I saw the Commissioner turn his head after studying me, whisper something to an official sitting beside him, make a disparaging gesture towards me, and then smirk at me as if I were a minor, amusing presence. I knew at that moment that I would brutally get at him with all the fight of a beleaguered "Jew-bastard" living as a tough child on 110th Street, East Harlem, rather than a civilized lawyer; that I would that day conquer and destroy my childhood tormentors, and most important, this personification of bureaucratic despotism who had determined to humiliate, arrogantly and publicly, a worthy and decent dead man, his family, and that man's defenders.

The hearing began. I must draw in part on news accounts in order to report that day objectively.

From the *New York Post*: "Before Lent opened the hearing, Kennedy, who was in the hearing room, began to take charge. He ordered the official stenographer to take down the names of everyone present, including reporters, T.V. and news-reel men."

The hearing was preceded by a sharp verbal exchange between the Commissioner and me. He assumed the authority to conduct this concluding hearing. I objected on the grounds that he had not been in attendance at the first hearing, that this hearing should be conducted by Inspector Lent, who had presided at the first hearing and who was familiar with the facts, and further that the Commissioner was interfering in and prejudicing a fair hearing.

The latter was an implied threat that I would go to Court again to attack the Police Card authority. The Commissioner angrily relinquished the hearing to Inspector Lent. I won that round.

I asked Inspector Lent that the Card be granted for Lord Buckley in compliance with the family's request and stated the reason for the family's request. I reviewed the Department's lifting the Card without notice and hearing, and Lord Buckley's record as a citizen, family man and performer, and finally, that my request be complied with "as a humane act." I did not call Harry Sedgwick as a character witness. I took less than five minutes in my simple and straightforward presentation.

Before Inspector Lent could rule on my request, Kennedy passed a note to Inspector Lent, who glanced at the note, frowned, and looked at me apologetically. "Denied."

I promptly asked for the note that had been passed and requested that it be marked in evidence on the grounds that the hearing officer's decision had been directed by the Commissioner, and further that the Commissioner had not attended the previous hearing and therefore was not familiar with the evidence. His interference was therefore prejudicial to a fair hearing. Kennedy reached for the note and deliberately tore it.

Now again, the *New York Post*:

> One of the spectators was Henry Dwight Sedgwick . . .
> who identified himself as a member of the Emergency
> Committee. Kennedy turned on him and began shout-
> ing one question after another. "Who are the Citi-

zens?" "What is the emergency," and "Were you ever known by any other name?" When he asked the latter question, Maxwell T. Cohen, attorney for Lord Buckley, shouted back "That was a stupid question and you should apologize for asking such a question. You make me ashamed you are a Police Commissioner of this City." [One of the other papers reported me as having added "You are a disgrace to the Police Department."]

"I don't need you to teach me how to behave," Kennedy snapped back. He continued to shout at Sedgwick who called it "harrassment."

I interrupt to observe that Kennedy lost a round to destiny at that point. At the end of this grueling day, I walked out of the room with Harry Sedgwick. I apologized for the inconvenience and the fact that he had been attacked by Kennedy.

"I should have told him that I was known by another name," said Harry. I stopped in amazement—now this on top of everything else! Harry continued, "The Kennedys call me 'Duke.'" "What Kennedys?" I asked. He casually replied, "Jack and Bobby. We've known each other a long time. Don't worry about today. I will take care of the Commissioner."

I learned later from a reliable source that Police Commissioner Kennedy was now excluded as a prospective successor to J. Edgar Hoover as Director of the F.B.I. (He had been considered as a replacement for the F.B.I. Director, whom the Kennedys intensely disliked.)

Now the battle began. What amazes me in retrospect is why the Commissioner did not leave the hearing room and so avoid the battle and its consequences. He remained in the room, fighting ferociously and being fought ferociously. The television cameras and press were eagerly recording everything that was said and done. That night, newscasts were extended an additional 15 minutes to report this event. The wires transmitted the events of the day to the press throughout the world.

There was drama: the powerful Police Commissioner of
New York City who had dominated the Mayor, the press, his
Department, and the City, was being fought and down-
graded by an unknown, unpretentious little lawyer who had
battled for a Card for a dead man. (*Down Beat* magazine
referred to it as the "battle of David and Goliath.")

Humes came in late, sized up the situation; he and
Kennedy then went at each other and outshouted each other.
Kennedy in desperation employed an unexpected tactic
which shocked everyone and embarassed his officials. He
suddenly reverted to Lord Buckley and began to read "this
man's criminal record." The press reported that I angrily
yelled, "You should resign for your own health. You are
obviously working under too much pressure."

From the *Daily News*: "Of charges that the cops transmitted more than $500,000 to the Police Pension Fund, Kennedy
said the amount is more like one million dollars." The
reporters and officials gasped. This was the first time it had
been acknowledged that the amount deposited was more
than the $500,000 previously believed to be the figure. The
Commissioner, aware of his damaging admission, lamely
answered (again the *Daily News*): "It's not material what
City pocket it goes into." This type of morality obviously
disconcerted the other police officials present and the press.

I was so tired. We had fought without any break for six
continuous hours. I noticed that most of Kennedy's staff had
slowly drifted out of the room and that those sitting beside
him at the table had, significantly, moved away from him.
Thus he was isolated and centered as a target. Deputy
Commissioner Reisman gamely remained to argue the law
with me, but, of course, he could not show explicit statutory
authority for the Police system.

After several hours of shouting by Kennedy and Humes,
Humes made an accusation that Lord Buckley had appeared
at the Police Department Honor Legion dinner gratis, and
that a bribe had been solicited from him at the dinner. I arose
from my seat to caution Humes not to make a charge which

could not be proven. I told Humes that if he made any charge, Kennedy would challenge him for instant proof. If Humes could not corroborate or support the charge at that moment, the Citizens' Emergency Committee would be attacked. (I later learned that there was some proof, but the witness had retracted under "advice.")

Kennedy taunted Humes to incite him to make wild statements. Humes, a skillful writer and a louder talker, aroused Kennedy to greater anger. It was at this point that a terrible and agonizing incident occurred. A television cameraman approached me, presumably to fix the microphone cord around my neck. He leaned over just as Kennedy's and Humes's shouting stopped momentarily. The cameraman was heard to say to me, "Give that son of a bitch what he deserves." The Commissioner heard this and so did others within a radius of six to eight feet.

I sank back and sat low in my seat, pained, depressed, and troubled. The next day the *Daily News* had a portrait of me looking as if I were in agony. The news photographer later apologized to me for the publication of the unflattering picture and explained, "You looked as if you were going to pass out, and that would have been a good news photo."

I no longer felt brutalized. I had a feeling of compassion for the Commissioner and earnestly hoped that he would now leave the hearing room. It was surely obvious to him and to all present that most of his staff had left and that the remaining few of his staff and the media people present enjoyed his discomfort. It was becoming increasingly apparent that he was no longer the strong and arrogant authoritarian official. Kennedy's own downfall and his humiliation were being recorded by the news media who had been assembled by him to witness his attack on the Citizens' Emergency Committee. It was a foregone conclusion now that he would no longer be invincible.

The experience was a tragic and bitter one for all. I never saw the Commissioner again. As I write this I feel contrite. I regret that day. I wish that it had never happened. I deplore the police system which dehumanized Kennedy, the callous disloyalty of his police associates, Humes's dramatic and fiery thrusts, and my own contribution to the Commissioner's fall and hurt.

The press began to hint that he would be removed, and I heard from a friendly city official that Mayor Robert Wagner had told him that "Kennedy got what he deserved. He brought it on himself." I was told confidentially that the Mayor was looking for an opportune moment to dismiss the Police Commissioner.

A paradoxical and driven man left public office hated by his Department and finally ignored by the press and the City. He moved to California. He might have been one of the foremost crime fighters in the United States, a credit to the concepts of law and order, but for one deficiency—he had never displayed a feeling of heart.

# CHAPTER EIGHT

Query: Can a group of seventy or eighty of the finest writers, editors, and publishers cope with civic problems? Can a group of internationally known intellectuals—"eggheads"—take on a corrupt system and fight?

Until two unfortunate incidents occurred—the famous writer stabbing his wife and the other writer whose traffic violations were exploited by the Police—the Citizens' Emergency Committee was becoming an unusual and forceful movement towards civic improvement.

Indeed, the Citizens' Emergency Committee startled the Mayor, who foresaw a repetition of the Governor Franklin D. Roosevelt-Jimmie Walker confrontation, interested the then Governor, Nelson Rockefeller, who had presidential ambitions, and disturbed the criminal powers in New York.

The Committee sent this telegram to Governor Rockefeller:

NEW YORK NY NOV 14 1960

GOVERNOR NELSON ROCKEFELLER

ALBANY NY

THE FOLLOWING PETITION IS RESPECTFULLY SUBMITTED BY THE PETITION COMMITTEE OF THE CITIZENS EMERGENCY COMMITTEE: WHEREAS THE LEXOW INVESTIGATION IN 1894, THE MOZET INVESTIGATION IN 1899, THE GAYNOR INVESTIGATION IN 1913, THE WHITMAN INVESTIGATION IN 1914, THE BUCKNER-CURREN INVESTIGATION IN 1930, THE SEABURY INVESTIGATION IN 1931, THE

AMEN-GRAND JURY INVESTIGATION IN 1938-
1940, THE KEFAUVER INVESTIGATION IN 1954,
THE BROOKLYN GRAND JURY-GROSS INVES-
TIGATION IN 1954, THE BROOKLYN GRAND
JURY INVESTIGATION IN 1959, THE CURRENT
INVESTIGATION BY THE QUEENS GRAND
JURY AND BY THE BRONX GRAND JURY IN
THE TOW CAR RACKETS AND OTHER INVES-
TIGATIONS OF THE POLICE DEPARTMENT OF
THE CITY OF NEW YORK ON FEDERAL, STATE
AND MUNICIPAL LEVELS HAVE CONCLU-
SIVELY SHOWN THAT ORGANIZED CRIME
COULD NOT AND WOULD NOT EXIST IN THE
CITY OF NEW YORK BUT FOR THE PASSIVE
ACQUIESCENCE AND IN CASES INDEED A
PROFITABLE PARTICIPATION BY OFFICIALS
AND PERSONNEL OF THE POLICE DEPART-
MENT OF THE CITY OF NEW YORK, AND
WHEREAS THE PROBLEM OF CRIME IN NEW
YORK IS THE SUBJECT OF CONCERN IN
THREE MAJOR PERIODICALS ISSUED THIS
MONTH, THE NATION, HARPERS, ATLANTIC
AND IN OUR DAILY NEWSPAPERS, THE HER-
ALD TRIBUNE INVISIBLE GOVERNMENT EDI-
TORIALS, THE NEW YORK POST SERIES ON
POLICY AND GAMBLING, THE NEW YORK
TIMES SALISBURY ARTICLES ON JUVENILE
DELINQUENCY, THE JOURNAL AMERICAN
EXPOSE OF THE TOW CAR RACKET, THE
CRIME EXPOSES BY DAILY NEWS AND DAILY
MIRROR COLUMNISTS THUS DEMONSTRA-
TING CONCERN BY THE PUBLIC IN CRIME
AND ITS DEVASTATING COSTS, AND
WHEREAS THE CRIME COSTS ARISING OUT
OF THE USE AND DISTRIBUTION OF NARCOT-
ICS IN NEW YORK CITY COSTS THE TAXPAY-
ERS OVER $200,000,000 ANNUALLY, AND
WHEREAS THE POLICE DEPARTMENT IS CUR-
RENTLY INVOLVED IN A BITTER INTERNEC-
INE WARFARE TO THE DETRIMENT OF THE

PUBLIC GENERALLY AND AUTO OWNERS SPECIFICALLY, AND WHEREAS THE POLICE DEPARTMENT HAS UNLAWFULLY IMPOSED WORK RESTRICTIONS ON EMPLOYEES IN CABARETS AND UNLAWFULLY IMPOSED FEES ON EMPLOYEES, AND UNLAWFULLY TRANSFERRED SUCH FEES AMOUNTING TO OVER $500,000 INTO THE POLICE PENSION FUND WHICH HAS UNLAWFULLY ACCEPTED SUCH FUNDS WHILE THE POLICE MEAN-WHILE PURSUE A POLICY ANTAGONISTIC TO CONSTITUTIONAL RIGHTS AND STATE PUB-LIC POLICY ON REHABILITATION, AND WHEREAS CRIME AND ITS COSTS IS OF PUB-LIC CONCERN ON A SOCIAL AND ECONOMIC LEVEL AND POLICE EFFICIENCY AND FIDEL-ITY IS INTEGRALLY INTERRELATED WITH PUBLIC WELFARE.

NOW, THEREFORE, DO WE CITIZENS OF THE CITY OF NEW YORK, RESPECTFULLY PETITION HIS EXCELLENCY, THE GOVERNOR OF THE STATE OF NEW YORK, THAT THERE BE APPOINTED WITH IMMEDIATE EXPEDI-ENCY A SPECIAL AUTHORITY EMPOWERED AND ENABLED TO: 1. INVESTIGATE, EXAM-INE AND DETERMINE THE EFFECT OF ANY AND ALL ILLEGAL ACTIVITIES OF THE PO-LICE DEPARTMENT OF NEW YORK, ITS PRES-ENT PERSONNEL AND FORMER PERSONNEL. 2. INVESTIGATE, EXAMINE AND DETERMINE THE ADMINISTRATION, OPERATION AND EN-FORCEMENT OF EXISTING POLICE RULES, REGULATIONS, PROCEDURES AND RELE-VANT STATUTES. 3. IN ADDITION THERETO TO INVESTIGATE, EXPLORE AND EXAMINE SUCH OTHER AREAS RELATED TO THE PROB-LEMS OF CRIME AND LAW ENFORCEMENT AS THE GOVERNOR OF THE STATE OF NEW YORK SHALL DEEM FEASIBLE. 4. TO PROSE-CUTE IN THE NAME OF THE PEOPLE OF THE

STATE OF NEW YORK WHERE EVIDENCE OF
CRIME AND CRIMINAL CONSPIRACY AND
COLLUSION IS DISCOVERED.

> HAROLD HUMES CHAIR-
> MAN PETITION COMMIT-
> TEE OF THE CITIZENS
> EMERGENCY COMMITTEE
> 250 WEST 94 ST. NYC.
> HENRY DWIGHT SEDG-
> WICK, JASON EPSTEIN,
> LLOYD MCKIM GARRISON,
> DAVID SOLOMON, MAX-
> WELL T. COHEN.

My letter to the Governor summarizes the developments.

November 30th, 1960

Governor Nelson A. Rockefeller
Albany, New York

Dear Governor Rockefeller:

May I as Chief Attorney for the Citizens' Emergency
Committee, write you concerning the contents of the
letter sent you by Mayor Robert Wagner and reported
in the metropolitan press on November 29th, 1960.

I did not see a copy of the letter in its entirety, but
have been able to reconstruct the substance of the letter
from newspaper reports and quotations. My references
may, therefore, be necessarily limited to that material
which was published.

(1) May I discuss Commissioner Kaplan's investigation first. [Kaplan was New York City's Commissioner
of Investigation.]

Commissioner Kaplan was a judge of great integrity
and ability and is unquestionably motivated by a desire

to render the best possible services in this instant situation. He was handicapped and this allegation is easily supported by what is now common knowledge.

When Commissioner Kaplan's investigators were looking for the very vital witness, Mr. Wintner [an agent who booked performers at cabarets], they were not informed, nor was Commissioner Kaplan informed that the witness was, for several hours, in conference at the Police Department. Had Commissioner Kaplan been able to interview the witness first the Commissioner would then have been able to obtain an objective and realistic report of what had actually occurred.

The failure by the Police Commissioner to notify Commissioner Kaplan of the immediate availability of Mr. Wintner, resulted in an unnecessary delay for Commissioner Kaplan of at least one complete day, contradictory stories by various witnesses, the need for obtaining additional evidence which again consumed several days—all of which could have been immediately avoided had the Police Commissioner seen fit to recognize Mayor Wagner's instructions to Commissioner Kaplan to commence investigation, that very day.

The very fact that Mr. Wintner's statements were contradictory gives rise to the assumption that there may be subornation of perjury by some interested party within the Police Department. Further, Commissioner Kaplan needed the willing cooperation and assistance of performers, musicians, cabaret employees and the cabarets. Before Commissioner Kaplan could make overtures to these citizens, and establishments, to induce them to cooperate, every cabaret in the City was subjected to an immediate, vigorous examination and inspection, by the Police Dept.

The message to the cabarets was obvious and unmistakable—the cabaret owner lives in a realistic world. The interpretation of the Police Commissioner's action was that the immediate and severe inspections and harassment were but a preliminary reprisal with greater reprisals to come. Significantly, the most vigorous inspection did not disclose any severe violation of law. Minor regulations were treated with such severity, as to create editorial comment and radio comment.

In this respect it is interesting to note the allegation made in the Daily News of November 30th, 1960, in which detectives indicated that a quota was set for additional inspections because additional violations were sought as a means of intimidation.

To the credit of the Cabaret owner, let it be stated that instead of being intimidated, he did the unprecedented act of applying for stays in the Supreme Court—and all stays were granted. But, in any event, as a result of this vindictive tactic by the Police Commissioner, the Commissioner of Investigation was deprived of the opportunity of obtaining assistance from that industry whose relationship with the Police Department is so close, that the police are referred to—without affection—as "my partners."

Possibly Commissioner Kaplan himself might be able to advise you in what other respects his investigation was handicapped by the conduct of the Police Commissioner and his Department. Suffice it to say, Commissioner Kaplan's report to Mayor Wagner was not the objective and thorough report and investigation that Commissioner Kaplan is well capable of making under better circumstances, and with cooperation. The Mayor's letter to you is necessarily limited by Commissioner Kaplan's report, and Commissioner Kaplan's report was necessarily circumscribed and inhibited by the damaging tactics and intimidating conduct of the Police Commissioner and his Department.

Bluntly stated, Mr. Governor, the Police Commissioner by these deplorable tactics thwarted any proper investigation by the Mayor of the City of New York, and the Commissioner of Investigation acting on behalf of the Mayor.

In all fairness, the skepticism that has greeted the Mayor's report should not be deemed a reflection on the integrity and conscientiousness of the Mayor and Commissioner Kaplan.

(2) With regard to Mayor Wagner's alleged legal basis for the Cabaret Employee's Identification Card, may I respectfully make the following observations:

There is no statute in existence, nor has there ever been any statute which expressly gives to the Police Commissioner designated, specific, unequivocal or clear authority with regard to the "licensing" of prospective or present Cabaret Employees, or the power to set forth the qualifications or disqualifications of present or prospective employees for such employment, or the right to impose "service charges" on prospective or present Cabaret Employees for Cabaret Employee's Identification Cards, or permission to dispose of such funds so obtained to the Police Pension Fund, or any fund not authorized to receive such funds.

The Mayor made reference to Section 436 of the City Charter. This section pertains to the Police Commissioner's powers over certain trades. The Police Commissioner is given the power to issue, revoke and suspend licenses for cabarets * * * and to make such rules and regulations for the supervision of cabarets— "as are not inconsistent with any other provision of law"—and power of general supervision and inspection "over all licensed or unlicensed pawnbrokers, vendors, junkshop keepers, junk boatmen, cartmen, dealers in secondhand merchandise and auctioneers within the city; and in connection with the performance of any police duties he shall have power to examine such persons, their clerks and employees and their books, business premises and any articles of merchandise in their possession."

I respectfully ask you to note, sir, that there is no specific reference to Cabaret Employees as such, and that the employees listed pertain to certain specified trades, and that the authority with regard to these employees is merely to examine, but not to license or to qualify, or to set conditions and fees as a condition of employment.

Any ambiguity is immediately removed by the remainder of the statute which reads:

"A refusal or neglect to comply in any respect with the provisions of this section on the part of any pawnbroker, vendor, junkshop keeper, junk boatman, cartman, dealer in secondhand merchandise or auctioneer, or any clerk or employee of any thereof, shall be triable by a city magistrate and punishable by not more than thirty days' imprisonment, or by a fine of not more than fifty dollars, or both. (As amended by L.D. 1947, No. 39, June 3.)"

It will be noted that again the reference as to clerks and employees of designated and specific trades is made, but there is no reference to the Cabaret Employee in that provision.

The Mayor makes reference to Section 436-1.0 of the Administrative Code pertaining to Cabarets. The presumption is that the $2.00 fee is authorized by that statute. This is incorrect. The fees fixed by that statute are as follows:

"1. The license herein prescribed shall be issued by the commissioner. Application for such license shall be made on a form containing such information as may be determined by the commissioner, and shall be sworn to by the applicant. The fee for such cabaret or public dance hall license shall be one hundred fifty dollars for each year or fraction thereof and for each such catering establishment license shall be seventy-five dollars for each year or shall be seventy-five dollars for each year or fraction thereof, provided, however, that a seasonal cabaret or public dance hall license may be issued for the period commencing on the first day of April and ending on the thirtieth day of September, for which the fee shall be one hundred dollars."

It will be noted, Mr. Governor, that the statute does not authorize the imposition of any fee by the Police Department to any employee. Such fees as can be imposed are the conventional license fees to the establishment only.

The Mayor further made reference to the Police Pension Fund. The composition of the Police Pension Fund is specifically fixed by statute and is governed by Title B18-3.0. The relevant portions pertaining exclusively to the Division of Licenses (of the Administrative Code) reads as follows:

"The Police Pension Fund shall consist of the following: . . . .

7. All moneys received or deprived from the granting or issuing of licenses to have and possess pistols or revolvers in dwellings or places of business, or to have and carry a concealed pistol or revolver * * *

8. All moneys received or deprived from the granting or issuing of permits or the granting of permission to conduct masked or fancy dress balls in the city. Such balls shall be conducted only upon condition that a license fee therefore of not less than five dollars or more than one hundred dollars shall first be paid to such department for the benefit of such fund."

The right to work is a common law and constitutional right of a citizen. Any statute or official act which seeks to diminish that right must be strictly construed as against that Agency, or against the official asserting the authority.

A proper reading of the statutes indicated by the Mayor will clearly show the absence of any expressed authority to the Police Department with regard to Cabaret Employees, fees to be charged, etc.

(3) With regard to the Mayor's deprecating "the general allegations," may I make the following observations:

Currently the Journal-American, and at times the World Telegram & Sun, are exposing the tow car racket and the Police Officers' profitable association with this racket. This is a current problem.

A few months ago—sufficiently few to be current, the New York Post published a discerning series of articles which exposed the police alliance with the numbers racket and the allied crime areas associated with the numbers racket. The columnists for the Daily News and the Daily Mirror make pointed references to illegal situations existing in the City.

A distinguished columnist for the Herald Tribune has repeatedly conducted a campaign, even current, with regard to the muggers, tramps and perverts harassing citizens in the area of Central Park. The Herald Tribune has published its magnificent "invisible government" editorials. The New York Times covers current crime analytically.

There are three current magazines, of great stature, The Nation, Harpers and The Atlantic, containing in their present issues articles on crime in the City of New York.

In the face of this exceedingly impressive and public evidence of corruption and police ineptitude, how is it possible for the Mayor to write you that the general allegations of corruption are "entirely unsubstantiated, utterly lacking in factual foundation and supported by nothing other than references to earlier investigations."

The Mayor will shortly prepare the City Budget. He will surely note that the narcotics problem never realistically faced in the City of New York will cost the

City of New York over two hundred million dollars annually in hospital, court, police and welfare costs. This problem is contemporaneous and this problem exists because as was pointed out by the previous Joint Legislative Reports and the Reports of the Attorney Generals of the State of New York, the narcotics problem thrives in New York, and it can only be sustained in New York by police passivity.

The plight of any citizen or citizen-group making a complaint is an ordeal. He is viciously attacked and maligned and made to feel that *he* is the object of an investigation. The Citizens' Emergency Committee comprises many distinguished writers, publishers and lawyers, some of whom are known to you personally. One of our members was accused by the Deputy Police Commissioner in charge of community relations of having twice refused to testify before a Grand Jury, when in fact at no time in his life had he ever been asked to appear before any Grand Jury under any circumstances.

Radio, television and newspaper reporters were told that the Chairman and Chief Counsel for the Committee had refused to appear at the Office of the Commissioner of Investigation, when in fact they had communicated with the Investigation Commissioner's Office, upon receipt of telegrams and made themselves available if requested to come down even by telephone, and had even written to the Commissioner of Investigation upon receipt of the telegrams expressing willingness to confer with the Commissioner. In today's Herald Tribune there is a very broad intimation that the Chairman of the Citizens' Emergency Committee would be brought before the Grand Jury for perjury— an obvious attempt to embarrass him on a thoroughly baseless charge.

The Police Commissioner of the City of New York forgetting his dignity, the importance of his position, saw fit to publicly interrogate a distinguished member of our Committee, I believe known to you personally, by snarling at him "Under what other names are you known?"

The Police Commissioner sought to humiliate our Chairman and me in a bizarre public spectacle which discredited him and also contributed to one of the tawdriest episodes in the current sorrowful state of our City.

Possibly more is involved here than the question of rights of entertainers, musicians, waiters and other Cabaret Employees.

Possibly, it is now time for the citizens of this great City to feel that the moral voice of the community now lies with the Governor of the State of New York. Our Courts, our Bar Associations, our Churches, our civic and political groups have abdicated their responsibility. The only moral voice in the community now is the metropolitan press. The only courageous voice in the community is the voice of the news-gatherer doing the investigation and work which is more properly the function of the Police Department and other Municipal and State Agencies.

Is it not time, Mr. Governor, that the City of New York be returned to its decent inhabitants and their families?

Possibly and as a result of your courage in facing this situation for the decent people of the City, other communities throughout the United States may take renewed courage and strength to realistically face their civic responsibilities and make our country a healthy, vigorous, sane community instead of a sordid, cynical and depressed area of social and family waste.

Most respectfully,

Maxwell T. Cohen

MTC:RFF
c/c: Hon. Robert MacCrate, Counsel to the Governor

History could have been made—and changed!
One can conjecture what would have happened if the Citizens' Emergency Committee had not been aborted.

Would Rockefeller have succeeded to the Presidential nomination as Roosevelt had under similar circumstances? Would the United States—and the world—have accepted "intellectuals" as a dynamic and articulate force for public good?

In any event, our most famous writers, editors and publishers dramatically united for the good fight—on behalf of a dead entertainer and others with or without distinction, and did display both brain and muscle.

# CHAPTER NINE

It was obvious now that the Police Card system was dying. Union officials faithfully came up with a number of substitute proposals, but in every instance a law would have to be enacted making the hitherto illegal Police Card system legal.

Later, however, such a law was passed, sponsored by the very unions whose membership would be adversely affected. It was for the most part ignored by both employees and employers. The police avoided the issue by casual enforcement.

Finally, one day the Police Card system died by an act of legislation. The battle was over. Rehabilitated former officials could work, musicians and performers were no longer equated with criminals.

Mozart was once employed by the Bishop of Salzburg, who insisted that Mozart sit and eat with the kitchen help as a social inferior. When Mozart refused to be demeaned as an artist rather than as a hireling, he was ejected from the palace. In the twentieth century, in the most prominent city of the world, a Police Department had arrogated to itself a right to humiliate musicians and performers and had deprived rehabilitated former offenders of their right to work. That shame was now ended, apparently forever.

We need not at this late date attempt to perpetuate in this book the disgraceful performance of the union officials. Needless to say, when the City Council repealed the compromise that they had sponsored, the unions loudly proclaimed in their house publications that each had fought and killed the Police Card system. No union, at any time, did anything to kill the Police Card system.

Joey Adams, the President of the American Guild of Variety Artists, and I had known each other for over fifty years. We had both come from East Harlem and from the same settlement house. He later explained to me his role in attempting to thwart my efforts to eliminate the system which was condemned by his own membership: "When one heads a union, one needs greater favors from City officials; sometimes one has to accommodate in order to be accommodated." A pragmatic reality covers all sins of action and omission.

Twelve years after the Police Card system had been eliminated, and six years after my law clientele had changed from musicians to other fields as a result of a new law partnership, I received a phone call which was a reminder that the Police Card fight was still remembered.

I was informed that for the first time in the history of jazz music, plaques would be awarded at the Newport Jazz Festival in Central Park for services to the jazz music community. Three recipients had been chosen: Father Norman O'Connor, the "Jazz Priest," a Paulist Father whose love for jazz music had given him a large following amongst musicians and listeners regardless of race and religion; Reverend John Garcia Gensel, the Pastor of St. Peter's Lutheran Church in New York City, where religious services often featured jazz music, and whose congregation included cabaret employees, musicians, performers, music lovers and their families of all religions and races; I was the third, notwithstanding the fact that my services, I thought, were of the past.

Jazz critic, author, and editor Dan Morgenstern made the public presentation: "Maxwell T. Cohen made it possible for thousands of musicians and performers and others to work, now and in the future, without fear and with dignity as human beings."

When I received the plaque, I saw the audience applaud. I heard applause behind me. I turned and saw that musicians had assembled on the stage and were applauding me. Tears came to my eyes. I bowed to the musicians. I bowed to the applauding audience.

I looked over their heads to the northern border of Central Park where Harlem, my birthplace and home for the first 18 years of my life, is located. I bowed to the two libraries on 115th Street and 124th Street, where I read as a truant and a high school dropout.

I turned to the northeast, in the direction of my childhood home, 110th Street, and bowed to the 110th Street Library and to the street of the early remembered sounds of the Italian funeral music procession, the old fashioned hand-wound Victrola, the Fischer piano, the children singing, the sounds of traffic, the screech and clanging of the 110th Street trolley, and the roaring sound of the Third Avenue E1.

These were the discordant sounds of life, the counterpoint to one's youthful private agonies, the overtones to adolescent dreams, aspirations, hopes, and escapist imagination.

I left the stage clutching my plaque.

**APPENDIX**

SUPREME COURT OF THE STATE OF NEW YORK
        COUNTY OF NEW YORK

- - - - - - - - - - - - - - - - - - - - - - - X

BERIL W. RUBENSTEIN, for himself and others
similarly concerned and situated,
JAMES LOUIS JOHNSON, for himself and others
similarly concerned and situated, and
JOHNNY RICHARDS, for himself and other
employers and taxpayers similarly concerned
and situated,

                              Plaintiffs,

           - against -

STEPHEN P. KENNEDY, as Police Commissioner
of the City of New York, JAMES J. McELROY,
Deputy Police Commissioner of the City of
New York in Charge of Licenses,
STEPHEN P. KENNEDY, JOSEPH J. REGAN,
WILLIAM V. COSGROVE, GEORGE BLUMENTHAL,
JOHN E. CARTON, LAWRENCE E. GEROSA,
BERNARD J. RUGGIERI, PHILIP H. GILSTEN,
JOHN J. CASSESE, VINCENT J. STEIN,
PATRICK H. FITZPATRICK, JAMES F. SHEA,
JOHN J. HORAN, Constituting the Board of
Trustees of the Police Pension Fund,

                            Defendants.

- - - - - - - - - - - - - - - - - - - - - - - X

> Plaintiffs
> designate New
> York County as
> the place of
> trial.

TO THE ABOVE NAMED DEFENDANTS:

               YOU ARE HEREBY SUMMONED to answer the complaint
in this action, and to serve a copy of your answer, or, if the
complaint is not served with this summons, to serve a notice of
appearance, on the Plaintiffs' Attorney within twenty days after
the service of this summons, exclusive of the day of service; and
in case of your failure to appear, or answer, judgment will be
taken against you by default, for the relief demanded in the
complaint.

Dated: New York, New York
      October 28th, 1958.

                            MAXWELL T. COHEN
                            Attorney for Plaintiffs
                            Office & P. O. Address
                            505 Fifth Avenue
                            Borough of Manhattan
                            City of New York

SUPREME COURT OF THE STATE OF NEW YORK
        COUNTY OF NEW YORK

- - - - - - - - - - - - - - - - - - - - - - X

BERIL W. RUBENSTEIN, for himself and others
similarly concerned and situated,
JAMES LOUIS JOHNSON, for himself and others
similarly concerned and situated, and
JOHNNY RICHARDS, for himself and other
employers and taxpayers similarly concerned
and situated,

                          Plaintiffs,

           - against -

STEPHEN P. KENNEDY, as Police Commissioner
of the City of New York, JAMES J. McELROY,
Deputy Police Commissioner of the City of
New York in Charge of Licenses,
STEPHEN P. KENNEDY, JOSEPH J. REGAN,
WILLIAM V. COSGROVE, GEORGE BLUMENTHAL,
JOHN E. CARTON, LAWRENCE E. GEROSA,
BERNARD J. RUGGIERI, PHILIP H. GILSTEN,
JOHN J. CASSESE, VINCENT J. STEIN,
PATRICK H. FITZPATRICK, JAMES F. SHEA,
JOHN J. HORAN, Constituting the Board of
Trustees of the Police Pension Fund,

                        Defendants.

- - - - - - - - - - - - - - - - - - - - - - X

        The plaintiffs, by MAXWELL T. COHEN, their attorney,
pursuant to Section 473 of the Civil Practice Act, and Rule 211
of the Rules of Civil Practice and all other appropriate and
relevant statutes, complaining of the defendants, respectfully
allege:

                  AS AND FOR A FIRST CAUSE OF ACTION
                  BY THE PLAINTIFF RUBENSTEIN AGAINST
                  STEPHEN P. KENNEDY, AS POLICE
                  COMMISSIONER OF THE CITY OF NEW YORK,
                  AND JAMES J. McELROY, DEPUTY POLICE
                  COMMISSIONER OF THE CITY OF NEW YORK
                      IN CHARGE OF LICENSES:

        FIRST: The plaintiff, BERIL W. RUBENSTEIN, at all times
hereinafter mentioned was and still is a resident of the State of
New York and was and is a Musician by training, skill and by profession.

SECOND: The defendant, STEPHEN P. KENNEDY, is
Police Commissioner of the City of New York.

THIRD: The defendant, JAMES J. McELROY, is
Deputy Police Commissioner in charge of the Division of Licenses,
a subdivision of the Police Department whose functions pertain,
among other things, to the issuance of Cabaret Employee's Identification Cards.

FOURTH: On June 21, 1957, plaintiff, RUBENSTEIN,
submitted an application, hereinafter referred to in "SIXTH", to
the Division of Licenses of the Police Department, for a Cabaret
Employee's Identification Card.

FIFTH: Upon information and belief, the Cabaret
Employee's Identification Card, as will be more fully shown hereinafter, is a document, which by direction of the Police Department,
must be obtained bi-annually from the Division of Licenses of the
Police Department of the City of New York with the payment of a
$2.00 "service charge", by all present employees, or those seeking
employment in any capacity, in establishments designated categori-
cally as "Cabarets", as a requisite to such employment.

SIXTH: The application form, hereinbefore referred
to in "FOURTH" was provided by the Division of Licenses. Such
Application form is annexed hereto and designated as Exhibit "A".
The following inquiry was made:

"7. (a) Were you ever arrested or
summoned (except traffic violation)?

(Yes or No)_____(b) If answer is
yes, state how many times and give facts_____."

In response, plaintiff, RUBENSTEIN, answered in substance that he
had been arrested, in Syracuse, New York, and subsequently con-

victed, in December, 1951 and September 1954, of violating Section
1751-A of the Penal Law, a misdemeanor, in that he had in his
possession marijuana, a drug, possession of which is prohibited
by the Public Health Law.

SEVENTH: The aforementioned Application for a
Cabaret Employee's Identification Card was immediately denied by
the Sergeant there in charge. No reason was stated.

EIGHTH: On September 9, 1957, plaintiff,
RUBENSTEIN, renewed his Application to the Division of Licenses
of the Police Department for a Cabaret Employee's Identification
Card.

NINTH: On September 9, 1957, the plaintiff,
RUBENSTEIN, also made application to the State Liquor Authority
(pursuant to Section 102, subdivision 2 of the Alcoholic Beverage
Control Law), for permission to work in the City and State of New
York.

TENTH: In order to obtain such permission, the
applicant, RUBENSTEIN, and his Employer or Booking Agent, executed
and submitted to the State Liquor Authority an Application form
and other supporting and corroborating data with regard to his
character, reputation, rehabilitation and readjustment. Plaintiff,
RUBENSTEIN, was personally interviewed by an official of the
State Liquor Authority and further investigated as to his fitness
to be employed in Cabarets.

A copy of the State Liquor Authority
Application form and a true copy of Section 102, subdivision 2
of the Alcoholic Beverage Control Law, are annexed hereto as
Exhibits "B" and "C".

- 3 -

ELEVENTH:  The petition and corroborating affidavits submitted by the plaintiff, RUBENSTEIN, to the Division of
Licenses of the Police Department, for a Cabaret Employee's Identification Card, on September 9, 1958, were in all respects the
same as those submitted by him at the same time to the State
Liquor Authority, for permission to work in the City and State of
New York.

TWELFTH:  True copies of the petition of plaintiff,
RUBENSTEIN, for a Cabaret Employee's Identification Card, together
with corroborating affidavits, certified copies of the Certificate
of Disposition of the aforesaid convictions issued by the Court of
Special Sessions of Syracuse, and other evidence submitted to the
Division of Licenses of the Police Department is annexed hereto
and designated as Exhibits "D-1" to "D-11" inclusive.

THIRTEENTH:a)The State Liquor Authority granted
the plaintiff, RUBENSTEIN, permission to work in the City and
State of New York.  A copy of this permission is annexed hereto
as Exhibit "E".

b)Such permission from the State Liquor
Authority has been thereafter continuously and consistently renewed and regranted to the plaintiff, RUBENSTEIN.

FOURTEENTH:  Prior to any decision or determination
by the Division of Licenses on the Application submitted by plaintiff, RUBENSTEIN, the Division of Licenses was notified that the
State Liquor Authority had approved plaintiff, RUBENSTEIN's
Application for employment in Cabarets in New York State.

FIFTEENTH:  Thereafter, plaintiff, RUBENSTEIN, was
requested to appear for a Hearing in connection with his request
for a Cabaret Employee's Identification Card at the Division of
Licenses.

- 4 -

SIXTEENTH: On October 15, 1957, a Hearing was conducted by Captain James O'Rourke, a duly designated Hearing Officer, in the Division of Licenses, attended by the plaintiff, his character witnesses and his wife, Jean. Detective Wallace acted as the Police Department's "Prosecutor".

SEVENTEENTH: The substance and essence of the testimony by the plaintiff, RUBENSTEIN, his wife and the character witnesses, relevant to these instant proceedings, pertained to the plaintiff's life after his convictions, his subsequent marriage to a professional Social Worker, his expectant fatherhood, his rehabilitation, readjustment, stability, good employment record and good character and reputation.

There were submitted and accepted in evidence on behalf of the plaintiff, RUBENSTEIN, certified copies of the Certificates of Convictions issued by the Court of Special Sessions in Syracuse, New York, and the permission granted by the State Liquor Authority (Exhibits "D-  and "E").

There was no documentary evidence submitted by the Police Department on behalf of the Police Department.

EIGHTEENTH: The Hearing Officer, Captain James O'Rourke stated informally, at the conclusion of the Hearing, that he would recommend to the Deputy Police Commissioner, that a Cabaret Employee's Identification Card be issued to the plaintiff, RUBENSTEIN.

NINETEENTH: On November 18, 1957, over one month later, a letter was received by the plaintiff, RUBENSTEIN, from the Division of Licenses, Police Department, a copy of which letter is

annexed hereto and designated as Exhibit "F", wherein reference
was made to the Hearing on October 16, 1957, and which denied,
with no reason stated, the plaintiff's application in these words:

> "Please be advised that the
> decision of this Hearing is the
> disapproval of the application."

This letter was signed by CHARLES CROWLEY, Lieutenant.

TWENTIETH: In truth and in fact, the aforesaid
statement was inaccurate and misleading insofar as it purported to
state the decision of the Hearing Officer, when in fact this was
the overruling decision of the Deputy Police Commissioner who had
not been present at the Hearing.

TWENTY-FIRST: Upon receipt of the letter dated
November 18, 1957, denying the Application, plaintiff, RUBENSTEIN,
sought to purchase the Minutes of the Hearing at the official rate
of $1.00 a page testimony, and was informed by the Division of
Licenses that the Minutes had not yet been transcribed.

TWENTY-SECOND: Upon information and belief, the
Deputy Police Commissioner had overruled the Hearing Officer even
before the Minutes of the Hearing, upon which the Hearing Officer
had based his recommendation, had even been transcribed.

TWENTY-THIRD: On or about November 21, 1957, the
plaintiff, RUBENSTEIN, requested the Deputy Police Commissioner
that he review or re-review the petition and exhibits and all corroborating evidence and testimony of the Hearing. A copy of this
request is annexed hereto and designated as Exhibit "G".

TWENTY-FOURTH: There being no response to the
aforesaid request of November 21, 1957, another such request by
letter was sent on December 19, 1957 to the Deputy Police Commissioner.

<u>TWENTY-FIFTH</u>: Thereafter, a letter dated
December 23, 1957, from the Deputy Police Commissioner denying the
Application was received by plaintiff, RUBENSTEIN. A copy of this
letter is annexed hereto and designated as Exhibit "H". No reason
was stated then, or thereafter, for the denial of the Application.

<u>TWENTY-SIXTH</u>: Thereafter, plaintiff, RUBENSTEIN,
instituted an action in the Supreme Court of the State of New York
against STEPHEN P. KENNEDY, as Police Commissioner of the City of
New York, and JAMES J. McELROY as Deputy Police Commissioner of
the City of New York in Charge of Licenses, et al. The suit was
voluntarily discontinued by plaintiff, RUBENSTEIN, by stipulation,
so as to enable the plaintiff to renew his appeal to the Police
Department, and in order to facilitate the transfer of the Division
of Licenses' RUBENSTEIN file from the Corporation Counsel's Office
to the Division of Licenses for the requested review.

<u>TWENTY-SEVENTH</u>: The Deputy Police Commissioner
declined to withdraw or modify his denials, or grant to plaintiff,
RUBENSTEIN, a Cabaret Employee's Identification Card, Temporary or
Permanent, with or without conditions attached (Exhibit "I").

<u>TWENTY-EIGHTH</u>: Plaintiff, RUBENSTEIN, through his
attorney, then appealed, by telegram, dated August 12, 1958, to
the Police Commissioner, Stephen P. Kennedy, as follows:

> "Pursuant to provision of
> Administrative Code Section 436.10
> respectfully request review in the
> matter of the application of
> Beril W. Rubenstein for Cabaret
> Identification Card. Supreme Court
> action in this matter was withdrawn
> by stipulation. Applicant has State
> Liquor Authority permission for em-
> ployment. Now married and enjoying
> good reputation and status as proven
> by testimony of reputable witnesses in
> the Hearing conducted by License Divi-
> sion."

- 7 -

TWENTY-NINTH: The telegram was not acknowledged
by the Police Commissioner. However, a letter was sent by the
Deputy Police Commissioner on August 15, 1958, granting the plaintiff, RUBENSTEIN, another Hearing "if there is any new developments" (Exhibit "J").

THIRTIETH: Thereafter, on August 25, 1958, a re-
hearing was conducted by the Deputy Police Commissioner. The
plaintiff, RUBENSTEIN, testified, and was examined at great length
by the Deputy Police Commissioner.

The Deputy Police Commissioner examined
and interrogated plaintiff, RUBENSTEIN, with regard to certain
traffic violations in Syracuse, New York, notwithstanding that
such offenses are specifically excluded by the Department of
Licenses' Application Form (Exhibit "A").

The Deputy Police Commissioner re-
ceived in evidence, on behalf of the Police Department, and in
violation of the plaintiff RUBENSTEIN's rights, Departmental
Reports prepared by the arresting officers in Syracuse, New York.

Upon information and belief, the
Deputy Police Commissioner accepted as true, the contents of these
departmental reports notwithstanding the fact that these reports
were shown to be erroneous and obviously in conflict with the
Certified Copies of Disposition issued by the Clerk of Special
Sessions of Syracuse (Annexed as Exhibit "D-  "), and the official
Minutes of the Syracuse proceedings.

THIRTY-FIRST: Thereafter, on September 9, 1958,
a letter was sent by the Deputy Police Commissioner to the plaintiff, RUBENSTEIN, again denying the plaintiff's Application for a
Cabaret Employee's Identification Card; copy of said letter is
annexed hereto as Exhibit "K". No reason was stated for the
denial.

- 8 -

THIRTY-SECOND: Thereafter, on September 11, 1958, the following letter requesting a review of Appeal of the denials by the Division of Licenses, was sent to Stephen P. Kennedy, the Police Commissioner of the City of New York, on behalf of the plaintiff, RUBENSTEIN, by his attorney. The letter reads as follows:

"September 11th, 1958.

Hon. Stephen P. Kennedy
Police Commissioner of the City of New York
Broome & Center Streets
New York, N. Y.

Dear Commissioner Kennedy:

When notified on August 12th, 1958 that Deputy Commissioner McElroy had denied the petition of Mr. Beril William Rubenstein for a Cabaret Employees Identification Card, I sent you a telegram which read as follows:

'Pursuant to provision of Administrative Code Section 436.10 respectfully request review in the matter of the application of Beril W. Rubenstein for Cabaret Identification Card. Supreme Court action in this matter was withdrawn by stipulation. Applicant has State Liquor Authority permission for employment. Now married and enjoying good reputation and status as proven by testimony of reputable witnesses in the hearing conducted by License Division.'

Thereafter your office referred the telegram to Deputy Commissioner McElroy who then conducted a Hearing.

This morning I received a communication from Deputy Commissioner McElroy in which he advises me that he is 'forced to the conclusion that no further change should be made in the previous decision reached in this matter'.

Pursuant to proper administrative procedures, may I ask you to review this entire matter. The ultimate authority in this matter from an administrative point of view lies with you as Police Commissioner.

For the most part, the Police Department has relied on the Matter of Friedman v. Valentine, 177 Misc. 442, to sustain its authority with regard to Cabaret Employees Identification Cards. This case holds:

- 9 -

'Neither does the regulation auto-
matically disqualify for employment one with
a criminal record. The police commissioner
may in his discretion permit persons with
criminal records to be employed where he believes this may be done without endangering
public safety.'

This decision clearly indicates that the ultimate discre-
tionary authority lies with the Police Commissioner. The
standard, or criteria stated by this decision is whether
public safety would be endangered. With respect to this
criteria, may I advise you that the State Liquor Authority
has again renewed and approved Mr. Rubenstein's request for
employment in the State of New York.

All of the other objective factors which were presented
in this matter, including the testimony of reputable witnesses, clearly indicate that the petitioner today is a
stable and mature individual, married, father of a new
born child, and certainly represents no immediate or po-
tential threat to public safety.

I would very greatly appreciate, Mr. Commissioner, a
review of this entire matter and respectfully request
the issuance of a temporary Cabaret Employees Identification Card, subject to whatever provisions this Department
sees fit to impose.

Respectfully yours,

MAXWELL T. COHEN

MTC:RFF"

THIRTY-THIRD: There has been no acknowledgment
by the Police Commissioner or any official in the Police Department of this request.

THIRTY-FOURTH: The rejection by the Deputy Police
Commissioner of the petition of the plaintiff, RUBENSTEIN, for a
Cabaret Employee's Identification Card in evident disregard of the
preeminent State Liquor Authority's permission granted to the
plaintiff to accept work in New York City; his arbitrary refusal
to accept the recommendation of his own Hearing Officer who had
observed the plaintiff, RUBENSTEIN, his wife, a former Social
Worker, and reputable character witnesses, and who had actively

- 10 -

conducted and participated in the Hearing; the Deputy Commissioner's
summarily denying the plaintiff a Cabaret Employee's Identification
Card even before the Minutes of the Hearing conducted before the
Hearing Officer were transcribed for his review; the delay by the
Deputy Police Commissioner for over one month in reviewing the
petition after the Hearing; the refusal of the Police Commissioner
to accept the Appeal for review and his referral of the telegram
and Appeal to the Deputy Police Commissioner, thus designating the
Deputy Police Commissioner as an Appellate Authority over his own
decisions of denial; the Deputy Police Commissioner's improperly
receiving as evidence untested confidential departmental reports
by the Syracuse arresting officers, and his acceptance of the contents of these reports as true, notwithstanding the fact that the
Syracuse police records were erroneous and obviously in conflict
with the submitted Certified Copies of Disposition of the two
arrests issued by the Court of Special Sessions of the City of
Syracuse (Annexed hereto as Exhibit "D- "), and the Minutes of the
sentencing proceedings in Syracuse; the constant inquiry and references at the second Hearing to the plaintiff's traffic violations when these violations are specifically excluded from consideration by the Department of Licenses own form (See Exhibit "A");
the Deputy Police Commissioner's disregard of plaintiff,
RUBENSTEIN's evidence of rehabilitation, marriage, parenthood and
good employment records, all attested to by reputable witnesses;
the indifference regarding the undeserved hardships resulting to
the plaintiff's wife and new-born child living in New York City, as
a result of the forced separation necessitated by the plaintiff,
RUBENSTEIN's seeking employment, to support his family, outside of
New York City; the refusal of the Police Commissioner of the City
of New York to acknowledge or accept the Appeal for Review dated
September 11, 1958, all of the foregoing constitutes unreasonable,

- 11 -

oppressive, arbitrary and unconstitutional conduct and processes
by the defendant, STEPHEN P. KENNEDY, as Police Commissioner of
the City of New York and JAMES J. McELROY, as Deputy Police Commissioner of the City of New York in Charge of Licenses, to the detriment of and damage to the plaintiff, RUBENSTEIN.

THIRTY-FIFTH:  As a consequence of all of the
foregoing, plaintiff RUBENSTEIN cannot obtain employment, and is
prohibited, in fact, from obtaining employment as a Musician in
any Cabaret in the City of New York, the preeminent State Liquor
Authority permission granted notwithstanding.

THIRTY-SIXTH:  Upon information and belief, should
the plaintiff, RUBENSTEIN, seek to obtain such proferred employment
in the City of New York, pursuant to State Liquor Authority permission granted him, the Cabaret Employer employing the plaintiff,
RUBENSTEIN, without the required Cabaret Employee's Identification
Card of the Division of Licenses of the Police Department, would
be subject to charges and severe penalties by the Police Department.

AS AND FOR A SECOND CAUSE OF ACTION
BY PLAINTIFF JAMES LOUIS JOHNSON
AGAINST STEPHEN P. KENNEDY AS POLICE
COMMISSIONER OF THE CITY OF NEW YORK
AND JAMES J. McELROY, AS DEPUTY POLICE
COMMISSIONER OF THE CITY OF NEW YORK
IN CHARGE OF LICENSES:

THIRTY-SEVENTH:  Plaintiff, JOHNSON, repeats,
reiterates and realleges each and every allegation of this
Complaint hereinbefore designated Paragraphs "SECOND", "THIRD"
and "FIFTH" with the same force and effect as though herein fully
set forth at length.

THIRTY-EIGHTH:  Plaintiff, JOHNSON, at all times
hereinafter mentioned was and is a Musician by training, skill and
profession.

THIRTY-NINTH: On December 27, 1946, plaintiff, JOHNSON, was arrested on a misdemeanor, convicted and received a suspended sentence. This was and is his only arrest.

There has been no other arrest within the past eleven years, or since December, 1946.

FORTIETH: Prior to October, 1956, plaintiff, JOHNSON, had made several applications to the Division of Licenses for a Permanent Cabaret Employee's Identification Card, but these applications had been denied. No reason was stated.

FORTY-FIRST: On or about October 22, 1956, plaintiff, JOHNSON, renewed his Application and Appeal. Formally and informally the Division of Licenses was informed:

(a) That plaintiff, JOHNSON, had been arrested only once, in 1946;

(b) That he has been continuously married since 1947; that he had two children; that he owned his own home; that he was a member in good standing of fraternal organizations;

(c) That he enjoyed world wide prestige as a trombonist, conductor, composer and was under exclusive contract with Columbia Records as a Recording Artist;

(d) That during the past five years, plaintiff, JOHNSON, had been voted first place as the most outstanding trombone performer by all Critics Polls, Magazine Polls, Trade Polls and Popularity Polls;

(e) That because of television performances, radio performances, concert appearances, cabaret performances, record sales and performances both in the United States and throughout the world, plaintiff, JOHNSON, has been heard and is heard by many millions of listeners;

(f)  That in his public appearances and performances before college audiences, adult audiences, groups of all ages, both in the United States and the other countries in the world, plaintiff, JOHNSON, was and is publicly accepted and acknowledged as a representative American Negro Artist and a typical American family man and as evidence of the fact that racial strife is not typical of United States culture;

(g)  That, upon information and belief, at no time was public safety, community mores, or the individual listener's social behavior adversely affected or influenced by plaintiff JOHNSON's appearances or performance as an artist in any part of the world; and

(h)  That plaintiff, JOHNSON's performances in New York Cabarets did not constitute a public threat or menace to public safety any more than his performances in the larger New York theatres, concert halls and television studios.

FORTY-SECOND:  The Application for a Cabaret Employee's Identification Card, was,nevertheless, denied by the Police Department of the City of New York.  No reason was stated, despite the overwhelming and conclusive proof of the plaintiff, JOHNSON's character, and the international prestige which he has earned.

FORTY-THIRD:  The State Liquor Authority, in the interim, had favorably ruled that there would be no need hereafter for the plaintiff, JOHNSON, to apply to the State Liquor Authority for permission to work in New York, and dispensed with the need for further Applications.

FORTY-FOURTH:  Plaintiff, JOHNSON, then requested by telegram, a Hearing from the then Deputy Police Commissioner in Charge of the Division of Licenses.  The Hearing was denied, but on November 7, 1956, the plaintiff was then informed by the

- 14 -

then Deputy Police Commissioner in Charge of the Division of
Licenses that he would receive a six months Temporary Card, and
upon completing a condition, a Permanent Card would be considered.

The following letter was sent by the
Deputy Police Commissioner to the plaintiff, JOHNSON, through his
attorney:

"        (SEAL)

POLICE DEPARTMENT
City of New York
New York 13, N.Y.

November 7, 1956

Mr. Maxwell T. Cohen
Attorney at Law
505 Fifth Avenue
New York, New York

Re. James L. Johnson

Dear Mr. Cohen:

With reference to your telegram of November 2nd,
1956, concerning the issuance of a Cabaret Employee's
I.D. Card to the abovementioned applicant, kindly be informed that I have completed my review of the matter and
I have ordered that a six months temporary I.D. Card be
issued to Mr. Johnson. He is to submit a statement from
any New York City Hospital at the end of this six month
period, indicating that he has been examined thereat and
was found to be free of narcotic use. If after this
period there is no further criminal involvement we will
consider the issuance of a permanent I.D. Card, provided,
of course, that he has clearance from the State Liquor
Authority.

Very truly yours,

(SIGNED)      ROBERT J. MANGUM

Robert J. Mangum
Deputy Commissioner
Licenses & Juvenile Aid

gj                                                           "

FORTY-FIFTH: That plaintiff, JOHNSON, is not now
and never was a narcotic addict.

FORTY-SIXTH: The then Deputy Police Commissioner
was informed by the plaintiff, JOHNSON, through his attorney, that

no New York City Hospital could conduct, or had the facilities to conduct, the examination requested to determine whether an individual was free from narcotic use.

FORTY-SEVENTH: It was then suggested that the plaintiff, JOHNSON, at the end of the six months period, supply certification by a reputable physician.

FORTY-EIGHTH: Plaintiff, JOHNSON, in pursuance of the aforementioned letter, and at the end of the six months period, did present certification from a reputable physician. A Permanent Card was denied him. No reason was stated.

FORTY-NINTH: Plaintiff, JOHNSON, at the termination of every subsequent six month interval, renewed his Application for a Permanent Cabaret Employee's Identification Card, presented his medical evidence but was, nevertheless, denied a Permanent Card. He was instead issued a Temporary Card.

FIFTIETH: The State Liquor Authority, in the interim, had favorably ruled that there would be no need hereafter for the plaintiff, JOHNSON, to apply to the State Liquor Authority for permission to work in New York State, or New York City, and dispensed with the need for further applications.

FIFTY-FIRST: In the interim, the present Deputy Police Commissioner, JAMES J. McELROY, was appointed Deputy Police Commissioner in Charge of the Division of Licenses, replacing the former Deputy Police Commissioner, ROBERT J. MANGUM.

FIFTY-SECOND: On June 12, 1958, plaintiff, JOHNSON, appeared at the Division of Licenses, at No. 156 Greenwich Street, New York City, with a doctor's certificate. He submitted his request for a Permanent Card and annexed thereto his doctor's

certificate. The Officer in Charge then made several statements,
the substance of which is herein presented:

That there were changes made in the policy;
and that he had no authority to issue a Temporary Card; and that
the plaintiff, JOHNSON, was to see the Deputy Police Commissioner
at once.

FIFTY-THIRD: Plaintiff, JOHNSON, was on the aforementioned date interviewed by the Deputy Police Commissioner.
Plaintiff, JOHNSON, was told in substance, by the Deputy Police
Commissioner, that there are now "new policies"; new restrictions;
that doctor's certificates would not be acceptable; that plaintiff,
JOHNSON, would have to report to any New York City Hospital for an
examination, and then obtain a certificate from the Hospital that
he was not addicted to drugs; that upon doing so, a Temporary Card
would be issued to him, but that the Card would restrict the
plaintiff, JOHNSON, only to a particular and specific place of
employment.

FIFTY-FOURTH: Upon information and belief, the
New York City Hospitals are specifically prevented by policy from
accepting narcotic addict patients except if they suffer withdrawal
symptoms in conjunction with any other ailment, and this prohibition has been extended to the extreme where New York City Hospitals
refuse to examine any person for the purposes of ascertaining and
certifying whether or not the individual is addicted.

FIFTY-FIFTH: Upon information and belief, the
Division of Licenses of the Police Department knows, and has been
informed, that no New York City Hospital will examine any applicant
with a view of certifying whether or not he is addicted to the use
of narcotics.

FIFTY-SIXTH (a)  Upon information and belief, the
Police Department's Representative, JOSEPH L. COYLE, Deputy Chief
Inspector commanding its narcotic squad, testified at Public Hearings conducted by the State of New York Joint Legislative Committee
on Narcotic Study.

(b)  Upon information and belief,
in the widely distributed Second Interim Report of the State of
New York Joint Legislative Committee on Narcotic Study (Legislative
Document 1958, No. 16, dated February 10, 1958), in which reference
is made to the testimony of the Police Department's Representative
and other City Officials, the Legislative Committee reported
(page 25):

> "Commissioner Morris Jacobs of the New York
> City Department of Hospitals, testified before the
> committee that there are no facilities for adults,
> except ' * * * when individuals present themselves
> to our other institutions with extreme withdrawal
> symptoms and possible complications of other condi-
> tions like diabetes or nephritis, in addition to
> the drug addiction, we admit these people and take
> care of their conditions.'  Dr. Jacobs agreed that
> the general policy of the hospital system ' * * *
> is not to extend facilities for care or treatment
> of narcotic addicts.'  This policy has been estab-
> lished, according to the Commissioner, because of
> personnel shortages, lack of space, pressures for
> treatment of patients with other diseases where
> prognosis is more hopeful, lack of medical agree-
> ment on the optimum treatment for narcotic addicts,
> sociological components of the narcotic problem,
> and many other reasons."

FIFTY-SEVENTH:  Upon information and belief, the
Division of Licenses of the Police Department notwithstanding this
knowledge, nevertheless deliberately demanded that plaintiff,
JOHNSON and other applicants obtain such impossible examination
and certification from any New York City Hospital as a means of
discouraging an Application for a Cabaret Employee's Identification
Card by any applicant who had ever been convicted of any narcotic
offense, no matter how remote in time.

- 18 -

FIFTY-EIGHTH: Plaintiff, JOHNSON, when interviewed by the Deputy Police Commissioner, was engaged to perform at "Small's Paradise" for one week and was, therefore, restricted to that place of employment by the Temporary Employee's Identification Card (See Exhibit "L").

FIFTY-NINTH: Plaintiff, JOHNSON's services were requested by "Birdland", "Village Vanguard", "Cafe Bohemia" "The Continental" and other well known Cabarets. Plaintiff, JOHNSON, was unable to accept any of the aforementioned engagements because of the practical impossibility of constantly applying to any New York City Hospital for an examination which could not be conducted, for certification which could not be issued, as a condition precedent to the issuance of a Temporary Card which even, if granted, would restrict him only to a particular and designated cabaret for employment.

SIXTIETH: Because of the oppressive, unconstitutional and unlawful proceedings by the Division of Licenses, as aforementioned, plaintiff, JOHNSON, is excluded from performing in cabarets in New York City and from engaging other musicians to perform with him in the Cabarets in New York City.

SIXTY-FIRST: Plaintiff, JOHNSON, is damaged in that he is barred from performing in Cabarets in New York City by the Deputy Police Commissioner. It is necessary, in order to maintain and support his family, for plaintiff, JOHNSON, to make constant tours throughout the United States and Europe, living separate and apart from his wife and growing children.

AS AND FOR A THIRD CAUSE OF ACTION
BY PLAINTIFF RUBENSTEIN FOR HIMSELF
AND OTHERS SIMILARLY CONCERNED AND
SITUATED, BY PLAINTIFF JAMES LOUIS
JOHNSON FOR HIMSELF AND OTHERS
SIMILARLY CONCERNED AND SITUATED,
AND PLAINTIFF RICHARDS FOR HIMSELF
AND OTHERS SIMILARLY CONCERNED AND
SITUATED AGAINST STEPHEN P. KENNEDY
AS POLICE COMMISSIONER OF THE CITY
OF NEW YORK AND JAMES J. McELROY,
AS DEPUTY POLICE COMMISSIONER OF
THE CITY OF NEW YORK IN CHARGE OF
LICENSES.

SIXTY-SECOND: Plaintiff, RUBENSTEIN, repeats, reiterates and realleges each and every allegation contained in Paragraphs "FIRST", "SECOND", "THIRD" and "FIFTH", with the same force and effect as though herein fully set forth at length.

SIXTY-THIRD: Plaintiff, JOHNSON, repeats, reiterates and realleges each and every allegation contained in Paragraphs "SECOND", "THIRD", "FIFTH", "THIRTY-SEVENTH" to "SIXTY-FIRST" inclusive, with the same force and effect as though herein fully set forth at length.

SIXTY-FOURTH: Plaintiff, RICHARDS, repeats, reiterates and realleges each and every allegation contained in Paragraphs "SECOND", "THIRD" and "FIFTH" with the same force and effect as though herein fully set forth at length.

SIXTY-FIFTH: Plaintiff, RUBENSTEIN, institutes this action for himself and on behalf of the more than

231 applicants and petitioners for a Cabaret Employee's Identification Card whose applications and petitions were formally denied in 1951 and years earlier, and for the

234 applicants and petitioners for a Cabaret Employee's Identification Card whose applications and petitions were formally denied in 1952, and for the

260 applicants and petitioners for a Cabaret Employee's

- 20 -

Identification Card whose applications and petitions
were formally denied in 1953; for the

293 applicants and petitioners for a Cabaret Employee's
Identification Card whose applications and petitions
were formally denied in 1954; the

304 applicants and petitioners for a Cabaret Employee's
Identification Card whose applications and petitions
were formally denied in 1955; the

328 applicants and petitioners for a Cabaret Employee's
Identification Card whose applications were formally
denied in 1956; the

334 applicants and petitioners for a Cabaret Employee's
Identification Card whose applications and petitions
were formally denied in 1957

and on behalf of those whose applications and petitions were
formally denied thus far for the year 1958, and on behalf of the
thousands of other Cabaret Employees whose applications were
initially rejected pursuant to Section 5a of the Rules and
Regulations of the Division of Licenses of the Police Department,
as will be more fully shown, when they presented or attempted
to present their applications for a Cabaret Employee's Identification Card to the Division of Licenses of the Police Department,
of the City of New York, and whose rejections and denials by
the Division of Licenses are not included in the statistical
formal denials, supra, published in the Police Commissioners
Annual Report to the Mayor of the City of New York.

SIXTY-SIXTH: Plaintiff, JOHNSON, institutes
this action for himself and on behalf of holders of Temporary
Cabaret Identification Cards.

- 21 -

SIXTY-SEVENTH: That at all times hereinafter
mentioned, plaintiff, RICHARDS, was and is a resident of, and
taxpayer in the State of New York, and is by profession, training
and skill an orchestra Conductor and Composer who engages and
employs musicians and entertainers to perform for him and with him
in Cabarets, Theatres, Concert Halls and Recording Sessions, in
the City of New York and elsewhere.

SIXTY-EIGHTH: The plaintiff, JOHNNY RICHARDS,
institutes this action for himself and on behalf of all other
Orchestra Conductors, Cabaret Owners, Booking Agencies, Entertainment Units, Productions, and all other Employers similarly situated
and concerned, whose rights to employ musicians, entertainers and
other Cabaret Employees is affected by the unauthorized operations
of the Division of Licenses of the Police Department with respect
to alleged Cabaret Employee's Identification Cards.

SIXTY-NINTH: Plaintiff, RICHARDS, has obtained
and is in possession of a Cabaret Employee's Identification Card
and institutes this action on behalf of holders of Cabaret
Employee's Identification Cards.

SEVENTIETH: Upon information and belief, there is
no provision in the City Charter, the Administrative Code of the
City of New York, or the Municipal Ordinances, which ever gave, or
now gives, to the Police Department authority for "licensing"
prospective or present Cabaret Employees, or the power to set forth
the qualifications or disqualifications of present or prospective
employees for such employment, or the right to impose "service
charges" on prospective or present Cabaret Employees for Cabaret
Employee's Identification Cards, or as will be hereafter shown,
permission to dispose of funds so obtained, to any Fund or Body not
authorized to receive such funds.

SEVENTY-FIRST: Upon information and belief, the duties of the Police Department, as outlined in Section 435 of the City Charter, did not contain and does not contain any provision or direction which gives to the Police Department clear, definite and unequivocal authority for "licensing" of prospective or present Cabaret Employees, or the power to set forth the qualifications or disqualifications of present or prospective employees for such employment, or the right to impose "service charges" on prospective or present Cabaret Employees for Cabaret Employee's Identification Cards, or permission to dispose of funds so obtained to any Fund or Body not authorized to receive such funds.

SEVENTY-SECOND: Upon information and belief, Section 436 of the City Charter pertaining to the Police Commissioner's Powers over Certain Trades did not give, and does not give, to the Police Commissioner designated, specific, unequivocal or clear authority with regard to the "licensing" of prospective or present Cabaret Employees, or the power to set forth the qualifications or disqualifications of present or prospective employees for such employment, or the right to impose "service charges" on prospective or present Cabaret Employees for Cabaret Employee's Identification Cards, or permission to dispose of such funds so obtained to any Fund or Body not authorized to receive such funds. The Statute reads as follows:

§436. Powers over certain trades.-- The commissioner shall in his discretion issue, revoke and suspend licenses for public dance halls, cabarets, hacks, taxicabs and taxi drivers, and make such rules and regulations for the supervision and operation of such public dance halls, cabarets, hacks, taxicabs and taxi drivers as are not inconsistent with any other provision of law, shall possess powers of general supervision and inspection over all licensed or unlicensed pawnbrokers, vendors, junkshop keepers, junk boatmen, cartmen, dealers in secondhand merchandise and auctioneers within the city; and in connection with the performance of any police duties he shall have power

to examine such persons, their clerks and employees
and their books, business premises and any articles
of merchandise in their possession. A refusal or
neglect to comply in any respect with the provisions
of this section on the part of any pawnbroker, vendor,
junkshop keeper, junk boatman, cartman, dealer in
secondhand merchandise or auctioneer, or any clerk or
employee of any thereof, shall be triable by a city
magistrate and punishable by not more than thirty days'
imprisonment, or by a fine of not more than fifty
dollars, or both. (As amended by L.L. 1947, No. 39,
June 3.)"

SEVENTY-THIRD: Upon information and belief,
Section 436 of the City Charter, aforementioned, is in derogation
of a Common Law Right protected by the Constitution of the United
States, and the Constitution of the State of New York - - the
individual's right to work, and therefore the Statute must be
strictly construed.

(a) Upon information and belief,
Section 436 delineates specific areas of control. The only references therein to employees ("Clerks and Employees"), specifically
pertains to these designated trades:

"'all licensed or unlicensed pawnbrokers, vendors, junkshop keepers,
junk boatmen, cartmen, dealers in
secondhand merchandise and auctioneers within the city.'"

(b) Upon information and belief, the
power of the Police Commissioner with regard to these designated
employees is carefully delineated, and the power is specifically
one of "examination" only, to wit:

" * * * in connection with the performance
of any police duties he shall have power
to examine such persons (licensed or unlicensed pawnbrokers, etc.), their clerks
and employees and their books, business
premises and any articles of merchandise
in their possession."

(c) Upon information and belief, even
the "punishment" is therein prescribed:- And incidentally, the

identity of the specific employees governed by the Statute is repeated:

> "A refusal or neglect to comply in any respect with the provisions of this section on the part of any pawnbroker, vendor, junk-shop keeper, junk boatman, cartman, dealer in secondhand merchandise or auctioneer, or any clerk or employee of any thereof, shall be triable by a city magistrate and punishable by not more than thirty days' imprisonment, or by a fine of not more than fifty dollars, or both."

(d) Upon information and belief, Section 436 aforesaid contains no reference whatsoever to the Police Commissioner's alleged power to "license" prospective or present cabaret Employees, or the power to set forth the qualifications or disqualifications of present or prospective employees for such employment, or the right to impose "service charges" on prospective or present Cabaret Employees for Cabaret Employee's Identification Cards, or permission to dispose of such funds so obtained to any Fund or Body not authorized to receive such funds.

SEVENTY-FOURTH: Upon information and belief, in its assumption of unlawful authority with regard to Cabaret Employee's Identification Cards, and in its disregard for the limitations set forth in Section 436, as aforesaid, the Division of Licenses assails the vital fundamental principle of law that statutes passed in the exercise of the police power of the state and infringing upon a common right, restricting and regulating property rights, or the pursuit of lawful occupations and callings must be construed strictly.

SEVENTY-FIFTH: Upon information and belief, Section 436-1.0 of the Administrative Code of the City of New York pertaining to the Regulation of Dance Halls and Cabarets, did not give and does not give to the Police Commissioner specific, desig-

nated, unequivocal or clear authority with regard to the
"licensing" of prospective or present Cabaret Employees, or the
power to set forth the qualifications or disqualifications of
present or prospective employees for such employment, or the right
to impose "service charges" on prospective or present Cabaret
Employees for Cabaret Employee's Identification Cards, or permission
to dispose of such funds so obtained to any Fund or Body not authorized to receive such funds.

SEVENTY-SIXTH: The relevant portions of Section
436-1.0 of the Administrative Code reads as follows:

> "b. Public dance halls, cabarets
> and catering establishments; license.-- It
> shall be unlawful for any person to conduct,
> maintain or operate, or engage in the busi-
> ness of conducting, maintaining or operating,
> a public dance hall, cabaret or catering
> establishment unless the premises wherein
> the same is conducted, maintained or operated
> are licensed in the manner prescribed herein.

> "1. The license herein prescribed
> shall be issued by the commissioner. Applica-
> tion for such license shall be made on a form
> containing such information as may be deter-
> mined by the commissioner, and shall be sworn
> to by the applicant. The fee for such cabaret
> or public dance hall license shall be one hundred
> fifty dollars for each year or fraction thereof
> and for each such catering establishment license
> shall be seventy-five dollars for each year or
> fraction thereof, provided, however, that a
> seasonal cabaret or public dance hall license
> may be issued for the period commencing on the
> first day of April and ending on the thirtieth
> day of September, for which the fee shall be
> one hundred dollars.

> In the event that an applica-
> tion for a cabaret, dance hall or catering
> establishment license is disapproved, a fee of
> twenty-five dollars shall be collected for the
> processing of the cabaret or dance hall applica-
> tion, and a fee of ten dollars for the processing
> of the catering establishment application."

<u>SEVENTY-SEVENTH</u>:  Upon information and belief, notwithstanding the absence of any statutory authority for "licensing" prospective or present cabaret or restaurant Employees, or the power to set forth the qualifications or disqualifications of present or prospective Employees for such employment, or the right to impose "service charges" on prospective or present Cabaret Employees for Cabaret Employee's Identification Cards, or permission to dispose of funds so obtained to any Fund or Body not authorized to receive such funds, the Police Department unilaterally created and does enforce certain unlawful and improper provisions contained in the Rules and Regulations of the Department of Licenses identified hereafter as L. D. 69.

<u>SEVENTY-EIGHTH</u>:  Upon information and belief, the specifically objectionable provisions read as follows:

"5.  Fingerprints of employees.  Every employee of a cabaret who comes in contact or is likely to come in contact with the patrons thereof shall, within three (3) days of the date of the original employment, make application and be fingerprinted at the Division of Licenses for a cabaret and public dance hall employee's identification card.  An employee of a cabaret conducted in a hotel of more than 200 rooms is exempt from this provision if the cabaret is conducted by the hotel management or ownership.  All individuals, members of a co-partnership and all officers of a corporation holding a public dance hall or cabaret license not participating in the physical operation of such licensed premises do not require an employee's identification card.

(a)  Except in the discretion of the Police Commissioner, no person shall be issued a cabaret and public dance hall employee's identification card or temporary permit who has been convicted of a felony or of any misdemeanor or offense, or is or pretends to be a homosexual or lesbian, * * * .

"6.  Identification card.  No person who comes in contact or is likely to come in contact with the patrons of a cabaret shall be employed on the premises of a cabaret more than three (3) days after the date of original employment, and shall not be re-employed unless such person has obtained a current cabaret and public dance hall employee's identification card

or temporary permit issued by the Police Commissioner
in such form and manner as he may prescribe. * * *
An employee of a cabaret conducted in a hotel of more
than 200 rooms, is exempt from this provision if the
cabaret is conducted by the hotel management or ownership.  All individuals, members of a co-partnership
and all officers of a corporation holding a public
dance hall or cabaret license not participating in
the physical operation of such licensed premises do
not require an employee's identification card. * * *"

"(1)  A service charge of $2.00 shall be
paid by the applicant at the time of applying for a
cabaret and public dance hall employee's identification card or a renewal of same.  In the case of a
lost identification card, an additional fee of $2.00
shall be charged for each duplicate card issued.  All
money collected for cabaret and public dance hall
employee's identification cards shall be forwarded
daily to the Bureau of Audit and Accounts for deposit
to the credit of the Police Pension Fund (Art. 1)."

SEVENTY-NINTH:  Upon information and belief, the
Division of Licenses Rules and Regulations 5, 5(a), 6 and 6(1)
aforementioned, are in any event void as class legislation in that
they subject persons engaged in the same business to different
restrictions and affords them different privileges, more specifically in that although purportedly requiring all Cabaret Employees
to be fingerprinted and to obtain Cabaret Employee's Identification
Cards, Rules 5 and 6 respectively specifically state:

"An employee of a cabaret
conducted in a hotel of more than 200 rooms
is exempt from this provision * * * if the
cabaret is conducted by the hotel management
or ownership."

and

"All individuals, members of a
co-partnership and all officers of a corporation holding a public dance hall or
cabaret license not participating in the
physical operation of such licensed premises do not require an employee's identification card."

EIGHTIETH:  Upon information and belief, there is
no statutory authority, other than that unlawfully self-assumed

- 28 -

under Section 5(a) of the Division of Licenses Rules and Regulations, supra, to bar homosexuals or lesbians from lawful employment in cabarets or restaurants.

EIGHTY-FIRST: Upon information and belief, the assumption of such unauthorized power as aforesaid by the Division of Licenses of the Police Department results in the deprivation of a class of citizens or residents not convicted of any offense, of their rights to lawful employment because of their incapability of, or disinclination for heterosexual functioning and is, therefore, in violation of their rights guaranteed by the Constitution of the United States and the Constitution of New York State.

EIGHTY-SECOND: Upon information and belief, in implementing the aforementioned unlawful and improper provisions of the Police Department L. D. 69, Sections 5 and 5(a), 6 and 6(1), the Division of Licenses of the Police Department requires all present Cabaret Employees or those seeking such employment (excepting those specifically excepted, supra, "SEVENTY-NINTH"), to apply for a Cabaret Employee's Identification Card as a condition to such employment, and to execute an Application, a copy of which is annexed hereto and marked Exhibit "A".

EIGHTY-THIRD: Although there is no inquiry made in the form as to whether the applicant was ever "convicted of any felony or misdemeanor or offense" (cf. 5a supra), the applicant is asked:

> "7. (a)  Were you ever arrested or summoned (except traffic violation)?
>
> (Yes or No)_____(b) If answer is yes, state how many times and give facts_____."

That consequently in violation of all known and accepted Common, Constitutional and Statutory laws, an arrest, which, per se is no evidence of guilt, is improperly made equivalent to a conviction of "a felony or misdemeanor or offense" by the Police Department to the detriment of the applicant and prejudicial to his rights to obtain lawful employment.

EIGHTY-FOURTH: Upon information and belief, if the aforesaid application indicates that the applicant was ever "arrested" or convicted, then in accordance with the usual and established procedure of the Division of Licenses, the applicant will then and there be told or advised by an officer on duty not to submit his application for the consequences of such submission will be a denial.

EIGHTY-FIFTH: Upon information and belief, the Police Commissioner's Annual Reports do not indicate how many thousands of applications have been or were thus arbitrarily rejected.

EIGHTY-SIXTH: Upon information and belief, should such applicant insist upon submitting his application, and in addition supply corroborative evidence of rehabilitation, or of good reputation and character, or a State Liquor Authority employment permission, such application may then be reviewed by a higher official for denial or approval, or for a scheduled Hearing by the Division of Licenses.

EIGHTY-SEVENTH: Upon information and belief, the number of applications, at least since 1951, formally denied after review, annually, as reported in the Police Commissioners Annual

Report to the Mayor of the City of New York is incorporated and referred to in "SIXTY-FIFTH" herein.

EIGHTY-EIGHTH: Upon information and belief, the cumulative number of applications formally and informally rejected and denied may now total over 5,000.

EIGHTY-NINTH: Upon information and belief, the arbitrary abuses inherent in the aforementioned procedure are not overcome by the introductory phrase to L. D. 69, subdivision 5-2 "except in the discretion of the Police Commissioner", since there never was, nor is there now any administrative machinery for an Appeal to the Police Commissioner, nor does the Police Commissioner acknowledge receipt of such an Appeal if communicated to him by the applicant or his attorney.

NINETIETH:a)Upon information and belief, the Division of Licenses of the Police Department is in conflict with the controlling and preeminent authority granted to the State Liquor Authority by the Legislature under the Alcoholic Beverage Control Law, with regard to employment by State Liquor Authority licensees of those formerly convicted of specifically designated crimes (Exhibit "C").

b)Upon information and belief, notwithstanding the approval and permission granted the applicant-employee and employer after investigation, by the State Liquor Authority, the Division of Licenses of the Police Department has declined, and does decline to permit such applicants the rights of lawful employment if the employee should nevertheless fail to obtain the Police Department's Cabaret Employee's Identification Card.

NINETY-FIRST: Upon information and belief the Cabaret Employee Identification Card procedures unlawfully insti-

tuted by the Division of Licenses of the Police Department are
purposeless, superfluous, unnecessary and needless amongst other
reasons because:

(a) The public interest is adequately
protected by reason of existing and effective controls, supervision and examination,lawfully established,amongst which are the
following:

United States Excise Tax Agencies;

The United States Director of
Internal Revenue;

The United States Social Security
Authorities;

The United States and New York
State Unemployment and Insurance
Departments;

The New York State Liquor
Authority;

New York City Alcoholic Beverage
Control Board;

New York State Bureau of Taxation
& Finance;

New York City Building Department;

New York City Fire Department;

New York City Board of Health;

New York City Sales Tax
Authority; and other security
authority including the

Federal Bureau of Investigation;

Secret Service;

Treasury Agents;

State Police and other Agencies,
and including on a local level
every police command from precinct
through and including headquarters,
including Special,Confidential,
Police and Detective Squads.

(b)  The Division of Licenses Rules and
Regulations are sufficiently effective to obviate the Division of
Licenses' recourse to the unlawful provisions of Rules and Regula-
tions 69, specifically 5, 5a, 6 and 6(1), as aforesaid.

NINETY-SECOND:  Upon information and belief, the
unlawfully assumed authority by the Police Department, in barring
plaintiff RUBENSTEIN, and plaintiff JOHNSON, and other persons
from lawful employment as aforesaid, is a punitive police measure
needlessly asserted when there is no present, threatened or
imminent violation of law and is, therefore, contrary to public
policy and in violation of Constitutional principles.

NINETY-THIRD:  Upon information and belief, the
Police Department's unlawful assumption of power as a "licensing"
agency over all prospective and present Cabaret Employees, with or
without criminal records, without Legislative Authority and in
consequent derogation of the preeminent State Liquor Authority
powers in New York State, and its assumption of the right to
summarily enforce its own enactments concerning employees and
prospective employees of cabarets, and its unlawful imposition of
a "service charge" and its improper diversion of funds so obtained to a fund not authorized by Statute to receive such funds
as will be hereafter shown, is oppressive, illegal and offensive
to the Constitutional principle which abhors within one authority
a police authority -- of the arbitrarily assumed right to legis-
late, to interpret, to enforce, to unlawfully impose a charge and
to improperly divert the monies so received to a Body or Agency
not authorized by law to receive such unlawfully obtained monies.

NINETY-FOURTH:  Upon information and belief, the
assumption of power as aforesaid, by the Police Department, violates the Articles of the Constitutions of the State of New York
and of the United States, which Articles in substance forbids

acts or assertive powers which deprives any person of liberty and
property without due process of law, in that by the exercise of
the aforesaid illegal powers the Police Department deprives plaintiff RUBENSTEIN, and plaintiff JOHNSON, and others, of the legal
right to earn a lawful livelihood through the proper use of their
skills; a right which is a property right given that very status
and significance by our competitive economic system and society
which permits, encourages and approves the lawful exchange of
services and abilities for proper compensation and gain.

      NINETY-FIFTH:  Upon information and belief, that
the said unlawful assumption of authority, as aforesaid, by the
Police Department, is in violation of provisions of the Constitution of the State of New York and the Constitution of the United
States of America in that the Police Department constituted as a
Penal Law Enforcement Agency of Government, violates the prohibition against ex post facto laws by adding to the original sentence
of criminal conviction of an applicant for a Cabaret Employee's
Identification Card, a punishment not contemplated by the
Legislature - - the deprivation of the lawful right to seek gainful employment after expiation of the charged offense.

      NINETY-SIXTH:  Upon information and belief, the
overwhelming common law fundamental principle "that one is presumed innocent until proven guilty" negates any assumption or
attribution of present unproven guilt, and rejects any concept
which holds that a once expiated offense carries with it a status
of criminal permanency, to be accepted as a presently existing
criminal status and to be projected as a future criminal status,
and therefore, the Police Department's unauthorized and assumed
power to bar from lawful employment former but rehabilitated offenders is in derogation of their common law and Constitutional
rights and is unlawful.

- 34 -

NINETY-SEVENTH: Upon information and belief, that the said unlawful assumption of authority as aforesaid by the Police Department is in conflict with the Social Welfare ideals controlling in the State of New York, and violates in addition the public policy of the State of New York, clearly expressed in Court decisions, that good moral character is determined by an applicant's qualities at the time of the submission of his Application and not by those other qualities which existed at a time remote to the Application, and which demonstratively have been corrected by the applicant's moral reformation and other favorable circumstances.

NINETY-EIGHTH: Plaintiff, RICHARDS, has endeavored to employ plaintiff RUBENSTEIN, and plaintiff JOHNSON, to appear as featured Artists with his Orchestra in appearances in New York City Cabarets.

NINETY-NINTH: Upon information and belief, in effect and in consequence, the Division of Licences of the Police Department's unlawful assumption of authority with regard to Cabaret Employee's Identification Cards for present employees and those seeking employment in Cabarets, with or without records of previous offenses, and its attendant arbitrary abuses of processes and procedures, its violation of Constitutional rights as aforesaid, its conflict with the preeminent State Liquor Authority permission, its disregard for public policy and Legislative enactments, has operated and does operate as a disqualification for lawful employment to the damage of the plaintiff RUBENSTEIN and plaintiff JOHNSON, and others similarly concerned and situated, as hereinbefore stated, and of plaintiff RICHARDS, and other employers similarly concerned and situated.

ONE HUNDREDTH: Plaintiff, JOHNNY RICHARDS' rights and the rights of other conductors and employers to contract with plaintiff RUBENSTEIN, and plaintiff JOHNSON, and other present or prospective employees, or those seeking gainful and lawful employment in New York City Cabarets, is prejudiced, threatened and impaired by the unlawfully assumed authority of the Division of Licenses of the Police Department with regard to the requirement that the possession of Cabaret Employee's Identification Cards is a condition for employment.

ONE HUNDRED FIRST: Plaintiff, JOHNNY RICHARDS, in common with other conductors and other employers, is damaged, in that he and they, have been and are, thereby unlawfully deprived of the economically productive and professional services and skills of gifted artists, performers, and the services of others, many of whom have written permission to accept such employment by the State Liquor Authority.

ONE HUNDRED SECOND: Plaintiffs RICHARDS and JOHNSON have no adequate remedy at law with regard to this Cause of Action.

AS AND FOR A FOURTH CAUSE OF ACTION
BY PLAINTIFF JOHNNY RICHARDS AND
JAMES LOUIS JOHNSON AGAINST
STEPHEN P. KENNEDY ET AL CONSTITUTING
THE BOARD OF TRUSTEES OF THE POLICE
PENSION FUND.

ONE HUNDRED THIRD: Plaintiff RICHARDS, repeats, reiterates and realleges each and every allegation contained in Paragraphs "SECOND", "THIRD", "FIFTH", "SIXTY-EIGHTH" through "ONE HUNDRED SECOND" inclusive, with the same force and effect as though herein fully set forth at length.

ONE HUNDRED FOURTH: Plaintiff, JOHNSON, repeats, reiterates and realleges each and every allegation contained in Paragraphs "SECOND", "THIRD", "FIFTH", "THIRTY-EIGHTH" through "SIXTY-FIRST" inclusive, and also "SIXTY-SIXTH", "SEVENTIETH" through "ONE HUNDRED SECOND" inclusive, with the same force and effect as though herein fully set forth at length.

ONE HUNDRED FIFTH: Upon information and belief, at all times hereinafter mentioned, the defendants, STEPHEN P. KENNEDY, et al, were and still are Members of the Board of Trustees of the Police Pension Fund and administer the Police Pension Fund pursuant to Section B18-2.0 of Article 1, Title B of the Administrative Code of the City of New York.

ONE HUNDRED SIXTH: That the plaintiff, RICHARDS, possesses a Cabaret Employee's Identification Card, and plaintiff, JOHNSON, possesses a Temporary Cabaret Employee's Identification Card, for which plaintiffs RICHARDS and JOHNSON, respectively, paid a "service charge" to the Division of Licenses, pursuant to the Rules and Regulations promulgated by the Division of Licenses of the Police Department, identified as L. D. 69 6(1) which reads as follows:

> "6 (1) A service charge of $2.00 shall be paid by the applicant at the time of applying for a cabaret and public dance hall employee's identification card or a renewal of same. In the case of a lost identification card, an additional fee of $2.00 shall be charged for each duplicate card issued. All money collected for cabaret and public dance hall employee's identification cards shall be forwarded daily to the Bureau of Audit and Accounts for deposit to the credit of the Police Pension Fund (Art. 1)."

ONE HUNDRED SEVENTH: Upon information and belief, there never was, nor is there now any authority in the City Charter, the Administrative Code, the Municipal Ordinances,

which expressly allows or authorizes the Division of Licenses of
the Police Department to impose a "service charge" of $2.00, or
any amount, for a Cabaret Employee's Identification Card.

ONE HUNDRED EIGHTH: Upon information and belief,
the only authorized fees related to Cabarets that the Division of
Licenses can impose, are those specifically set forth in Section
436-1.0, of the Administrative Code.

ONE HUNDRED NINTH: Upon information and belief,
Section 436-1.0 of the Administrative Code, contains no reference,
directly or indirectly, whatsoever to Cabaret Employees or prospective Cabaret Employees.

ONE HUNDRED TENTH: Section 436-1.0 of the Administrative Code reads as follows:

> "b. Public dance halls, cabarets
> and catering establishments; license. -- It
> shall be unlawful for any person to conduct,
> maintain or operate, or engage in the business
> of conducting, maintaining or operating, a
> public dance hall, cabaret or catering estab-
> lishment unless the premises wherein the same
> is conducted, maintained or operated are
> licensed in the manner prescribed herein.
> (Subd. b as amended by L.L. 1945, No. 28,
> June 25.)"

> "1.   The license herein prescribed
> shall be issued by the commissioner. Application
> for such license shall be made on a form contain-
> ing such information as may be determined by the
> commissioner, and shall be sworn to by the
> applicant. The fee for each such cabaret or pub-
> lic dance hall license shall be one hundred fifty
> dollars for each year or fraction thereof and for
> each such catering establishment license shall
> be seventy-five dollars for each year or fraction
> thereof, provided, however, that a seasonal cabaret
> or public dance hall license may be issued for
> the period commencing on the first day of April
> and ending on the thirtieth day of September,
> for which the fee shall be one hundred dollars.

> If additional rooms are to be
> used independently by the same applicant in the

same premises as a public dance hall, cabaret or catering establishment, the applicant shall indicate on the application the location of each and every room or space which is to be used for such purpose. In suchcase a separate license shall be required for each such additional independent room or space, and the fee for each such independent additional room or space shall be ten dollars.

In the event that an application for a cabaret, dance hall or catering establishment license is disapproved, a fee of twenty-five dollars shall be collected for the processing of the cabaret or dance hall application, and a fee of ten dollars for the processing of the catering establishment application."

ONE HUNDRED ELEVENTH: Upon information and belief, since the Division of Licenses in the exercise of an assumed authority does not require an employee executing an application for a Cabaret Employee's Identification Card, to take an oath, or to have the application acknowledged, or to have the application transmitted officially to any other Agency, Municipal, State or Federal Authority, the imposition of such unauthorized "service charge" on a Cabaret Employee is in violation of Penal Law §1826, 1830, Public Officers Law Sec. 67, and, in that property is taken without due process of law, as aforesaid, the Constitution of the United States and the Constitution of the State of New York.

ONE HUNDRED TWELFTH: Upon information and belief, even if the authority assumed by the Division of Licenses was lawful, the "service charge" of $2.00 imposed by the Police Department is in absolute violation of provisions of Section 67 of the Public Officers Law of the State of New York, the relevant portions are:

"§67. 1. Each public officer upon whom a duty is expressly imposed by law, must execute the same without fee or reward, except where a fee or other compensation therefor is expressly allowed by law."

"3. An officer, or
other person, shall not demand or receive any fee or compensation, allowed
to him by law for any service, unless
the service was actually rendered by
him; * * *"

"4. Money received by a
public officer, or which shall come into
his possession or custody, in the performance of his official duties or in connection therewith or incidental thereto, shall
be held by him in trust for the person or
persons entitled thereto or for the purposes provided by law and all interest or
increments which shall accrue or attach
to such money while in his possession or
custody shall be added to, and become a
part of, the money so held and no part
of such interest or increments shall be
retained by such officer to his personal
use or benefit, except legal fees allowed
by law for receiving and disbursing the
same, notwithstanding the provisions of
any general or special law."

"An officer or other per-
son, who violates either of the provisions
contained in this section, is liable in
addition to the punishment prescribed by
law for the criminal offense, to an
action in behalf of the person aggrieved,
in which the plaintiff is entitled to
treble damages. As amended L. 1932, c.
563, eff. March 31, 1932."

ONE HUNDRED THIRTEENTH: Upon information and
belief, there is no statutory authority in the City Charter, or
Administrative Code, or the Municipal Ordinances, which expressly
permits or allows the Division of Licenses of the Police Department
to divert funds or "service charges" so unlawfully collected, to
the Police Pension Fund.

ONE HUNDRED FOURTEENTH: Upon information and
belief there is no statutory authority in the City Charter, or
Administrative Code, or the Municipal Ordinances, which expressly
authorizes, or grants permission to, or allows the Police Pension
Fund to accept the accumulated "service charges" funds as aforesaid
from the Division of Licenses.

ONE HUNDRED FIFTEENTH: Upon information and belief, the composition of the Police Pension Fund is specifically fixed by statute and is governed by Title B18-3.0. The relevant portions pertaining exclusively to the Division of Licenses reads as follows: (Of the Administrative Code)

> "The Police Pension Fund shall consist of the following:.....
>
> 7. All moneys received or derived from the granting or issuing of licenses to have and possess pistols or revolvers in dwellings or places of business, or to have and carry concealed a pistol or revolver * * *
>
> 8. All moneys received or derived from the granting or issuing of permits or the granting of permission to conduct masked or fancy dress balls in the city. Such balls shall be conducted only upon condition that a license fee therefor of not less than five dollars nor more than one hundred dollars shall first be paid to such department for the benefit of such fund."

ONE HUNDRED SIXTEENTH: Upon information and belief, notwithstanding the fact that there is no statute which empowers the Police Department, Division of Licenses, to impose "service charges" for a Cabaret Employee's Identification Card, nor is there a statute which permits or directs the Police Department, Division of Licenses, to deposit such funds with the Police Pension Fund, nor is there a statute which permits or directs the Police Pension Fund to accept such deposits from the Division of Licenses, there was, nevertheless, unlawfully collected by the Division of Licenses from holders of Cabaret Employee Identification Card "service charges", and there was unlawfully deposited, at least since 1947, with the Police Pension Fund the following moneys so collected (Annual totals indicated):

| | |
|---|---|
| 1947 | $ 19,976.00 |
| 1948 | 8,073.00 |
| 1949 | 7,124.00 |
| 1950 | 5,892.00 |
| 1951 | 17,685.00 |
| 1952 | 10,480.00 |
| 1953 | 40,176.00 |
| 1954 | 20,056.00 |
| 1955 | 48,626.00 |
| 1956 | 27,968.00 |
| 1957 | 31,804.00 |

ONE HUNDRED SEVENTEENTH:  Upon information and belief, the amounts thus illegally collected and thus unlawfully deposited with the Police Pension Fund for the above mentioned years, in addition to those previously unlawfully deposited, and with accumulated interest, profits and earnings, may total about one-half million dollars.

ONE HUNDRED EIGHTEENTH:  Upon information and belief, the exact amount thus illegally obtained and unlawfully deposited can only be obtained by an Accounting by the Division of Licenses and the Police Pension Fund to the plaintiffs RICHARDS and JOHNSON.

ONE HUNDRED NINETEENTH:  The Plaintiffs for themselves and on behalf of other payees of the unlawfully imposed "service charges", and on behalf of all other taxpayers, seek  an Accounting from the Division of Licenses of the Police Department and the Police Pension Fund, and also seek to recover the return to all payees the money illegally obtained by the Division of Licenses and unlawfully retained by the Police Pension Fund, as aforesaid, and for an Order directing the Trustees of the Police Pension Fund to turn over to the City Treasurer, for public use and benefit, any of the monies so obtained by the Division of Licenses and the Police Pension Fund, which cannot be returned to the original payees.

WHEREFORE, the plaintiff, BERIL W. RUBENSTEIN, for himself and others similarly concerned and situated, and JAMES LOUIS JOHNSON, for himself and others similarly concerned and situated, and JOHNNY RICHARDS, for himself and other employers and taxpayers similarly concerned and situated, respectfully pray for the following relief:

(1) A finding, decree and judgment of this Court that Section 5 and 5a, Section 6 and 6(1) of the Rules and Regulations of the Division of Licenses of the Police Department of the City of New York, aforestated, are in violation of the Constitution of the United States, and the Articles of the Constitution of New York State, and are therefore unconstitutional.

(2) A finding, decree and judgment of this Court that Section 5 and 5a, Section 6 and 6(1) of the Rules and Regulations of the Division of Licenses of the Police Department of the City of New York, aforestated, are void, unlawful and ineffective.

(3) For an order permanently restraining and enjoining the Police Department, and any of its officials, divisions, departments, precincts or personnel from enforcing, implementing or acting in pursuance of Section 5 and 5a, Section 6 and 6 (1), of the Police Department, Division of Licenses Rules and Regulations.

(4) For an order restraining and enjoining the Police Department, or any of its officials, divisions, departments, precincts or personnel from interfering with or impairing employment contracts in pursuance of Section 5 and 5a, Section 6 and 6(1), of the Police Department, Division of Licenses Rules and Regulations.

- 43 -

WHEREFORE, the plaintiff, BERIL W. RUBENSTEIN, respectfully prays of this Court for the following alternative relief:

(5) That in the event the aforesaid Section 5 and 5a, and Section 6 and 6(1), be deemed valid and constitutional, for an order directing the Police Commissioner of the City of New York, and the Deputy Police Commissioner in Charge of the Division of Licenses of the Police Department, to issue forthwith a Cabaret Employee's Identification Card to the plaintiff, BERIL W. RUBENSTEIN.

WHEREFORE, the plaintiff, JAMES LOUIS JOHNSON, respectfully prays of this Court for the following alternative relief:

(6) That in the event the aforesaid Section 5 and 5a, and Section 6 and 6(1), be deemed valid and constitutional, for an order directing the Police Commissioner of the City of New York, and the Deputy Police Commissioner in Charge of the Division of Licenses of the Police Department, to issue forthwith a Permanent Cabaret Employee's Identification Card to the plaintiff, JAMES LOUIS JOHNSON.

WHEREFORE, the plaintiffs JOHNNY RICHARDS and JAMES LOUIS JOHNSON, for themselves and other holders of Cabaret Employee's Identification Cards and taxpayers similarly concerned and situated, respectfully pray of this Court for the following relief:

(7) For an order directing that the Police Commissioner of the City of New York Account to the plaintiffs RICHARDS and JOHNSON, as to all funds received by the Division of Licenses of the Police Department of the City of New York with respect to Cabaret Employee's Identification Cards.

(8) For an order directing that the Board of Trustees of the Police Pension Fund Account to the plaintiffs RICHARDS and JOHNSON, for all funds received from the Police Department or any other Municipal Agency or Body for Cabaret Employee's Identification Cards, together with accumulated interest, earnings and profit.

(9) For an order directing that upon the taking and statement of the said Accounting, that the Board of Trustees of the Police Pension Fund and the Police Commissioner of the City of New York, and the Deputy Police Commissioner in Charge of the Division of Licenses of the Police Department, return forthwith to the respective payees, or their estates, all fees paid by them to the Division of Licenses for Cabaret Employee's Identification Cards.

(10) For an order directing the Board of Trustees of the Police Pension Fund and the Police Commissioner of the City of New York and Deputy Police Commissioner in charge of the Division of Licenses of the Police Department, that in the event such applicants cannot be located, that the respective fees of these payees hereto collected for Cabaret Employee's Identification Cards by the Police Department of the Division of Licenses of the Police Department and retained by the Police Pension Fund, shall be forthwith turned over to the City Treasurer of the City of New York.

(11) The plaintiffs, BERIL W. RUBENSTEIN, JAMES LOUIS JOHNSON and JOHNNY RICHARDS individually, and on behalf of others similarly concerned and situated, respectfully pray of this Court that the Court grant the plaintiffs herein for them-

selves and for all others similarly concerned and situated, such other and further relief as the Court may seem just, equitable and proper all together with the costs of this action.

> MAXWELL T. COHEN
> Attorney for Plaintiffs
> Office & P. O. Address
> 505 Fifth Avenue
> Borough of Manhattan
> City of New York

STATE OF NEW YORK )
COUNTY OF NEW YORK) ss. :

      BERIL W. RUBENSTEIN, being duly sworn, deposes and
says that he is one of the plaintiffs in the within action; that
he has read the foregoing Complaint and knows the contents thereof;
that the same is true to his own knowledge, except as to the
matters therein stated to be alleged on information and belief, and
that as to those matters he believes it to be true.

Sworn to before me this

28th day of October, 1958.      *Beril W. Rubenstein*

MAXWELL T. COHEN
Notary Public, State of New York
No. 31-5744300
Qualified in New York County
Certs. filed with N. Y. Co. Clk. & R.
Commission expires March 30, 1960

STATE OF NEW YORK )
COUNTY OF NEW YORK) ss. :

      JAMES LOUIS JOHNSON, being duly sworn, deposes and
says that he is one of the plaintiffs in the within action; that
he has read the foregoing Complaint and knows the contents thereof;
that the same is true to his own knowledge, except as to the
matters therein stated to be alleged on information and belief,
and that as to those matters he believes it to be true.

Sworn to before me this

28th day of October, 1958.      *James Louis Johnson*

MAXWELL T. COHEN
Notary Public, State of New York
No. 31-5744300
Qualified in New York County
Certs. filed with N. Y. Co. Clk. & R.
Commission expires March 30, 1960

STATE OF NEW YORK )
COUNTY OF NEW YORK) ss. :

      JOHNNY RICHARDS, being duly sworn, deposes and
says that he is one of the plaintiffs in the within action; that
he has read the foregoing Complaint and knows the contents thereof;
that the same is true to his own knowledge, except as to the
matters therein stated to be alleged on information and belief,
and that as to those matters he believes it to be true.

Sworn to before me this

28th day of October, 1958.      *Johnny Richards*

MAXWELL T. COHEN
Notary Public, State of New York
No. 31-5744300
Qualified in New York County
Certs. filed with N. Y. Co. Clk. & Regs.
Commission Expires March 30, 1952

POLICE DEPARTMENT

CITY OF NEW YORK

## DIVISION OF LICENSES   F

# APPLICATION FOR A CABARET OR PUBLIC DANCE HALL EMPLOYEE'S IDENTIFICATION CARD

### IMPORTANT NOTICE

**Full and complete answers are required to each question. Any false statement made by the Applicant herein is cause for Disapproval of this Application.**

**Applicant must furnish 2 photographs (1½ inches square) of recent date.**

| DATE APPLICATION FILED IN PRECINCT | PRECINCT | PRECINCT SERIAL NO. | DATE FORWARDED BY PRECINCT |
|---|---|---|---|
| | | | |

Date of Application_____

Full True Name_____

(Print)

Professional or Assumed Name_____

(Print)

Address_____

Date of Birth_____

ALIEN
CITIZEN

Place of Birth_____

Race (Color)_____ Sex_____ Height_____ Weight_____ Hair_____

Eyes_____ Complexion_____ Social Security No._____

### CABARET OR DANCE HALL IN WHICH EMPLOYED

Name _____

Address_____ Occupation_____

1. (a) Are you presently employed in any capacity by the City of New York?

    (Yes or No)_____ (b) If answer is yes, state employment_____

2. (a) Have you ever made an appplication for a license or permit issued by the City of New York which was denied?

    (Yes or No)_____ (b) If answer is yes, state date and kind_____

3. (a) Have you ever held a license or permit issued by the City of New York which was revoked?

    (Yes or No)_____ (b) If answer is yes, state date and kind_____

4. (a) Do you now hold a license or permit issued by the City of New York?

    (Yes or No)_____ (b) If answer is yes, state kind_____

5. (a) Were you ever employed or connected with a so-called " Clip Joint " or " Speakeasy " ?

    (Yes or No)_____ (b) If answer is yes, state facts_____

(OVER)      L. D. 74

EXHIBIT "A"=FRONT

6. (a) Were you ever employed in a cabaret or public dance hall where the license was revoked?

(Yes or No)_____ (b) If answer is yes, state facts_____

_____

_____

_____

7. (a) Were you ever arrested or summoned (except traffic violation)?

(Yes or No)_____ (b) If answer is yes, state how many times and give facts_____

_____

_____

_____

_____

(Applicant's Signature)

## NOT TO BE FILLED IN BY APPLICANT

Identification Card Number_____

ACTION TAKEN: } Disapproved.
} Approved.

REASON FOR DISAPPROVAL:_____

_____

_____

_____

Date_____      _____

(Signature)

## TO BE FILLED IN BY APPLICANT UPON RECEIPT OF IDENTIFICATION CARD

DATE_____

RECEIPT OF EMPLOYEE'S IDENTIFICATION CARD IS HEREBY ACKNOWLEDGED.

_____

(Applicant's Signature)

_____

(Issued by)

EXHIBIT "A"=BACK

```
- - - - - - - - - - - - - - - - - - X

   In the Matter of the Petition

              of

BERIL W. RUBENSTEIN, Petitioner          NOTICE OF APPROVAL

For approval of employment
under Sec. 102

- - - - - - - - - - - - - - - - - - X
```

                    Please take notice that your petition for the

approval of the Liquor Authority permit or employment by


PLAYGOER'S CAFE, INC.          1281-6th Avenue
(Name of Licensee)             (Address of Licensed Premises)


New York, N. Y.                Pianist
(City, Town or Village)        (Nature of Employment)


Is hereby approved,

              This approval should be valid only for employment

by the licensee designated herein and only for the duties above

specified. Should there be any change in the nature of the employees

duties, or should the employee seek employment with another license,

written approval thereof must first be obtained from the Liquor

Authority.

                    Certified by FREDERICK C. BATHWELL

                    TO: PLAYGOER'S CAFE, INC.
                        (Licensee-Employer)

                    TO: 49 Grove Street, New York, N.Y.
                        (Residence of Petitioner)

                         STATE LIQUOR AUTHORITY

                         THOMAS E. ROHAN, Chairman

                         JOHN F. O'CONNELL, Chairman

Dated                JAW:rg
Sept. 10, 1957


                         EXHIBIT B

ALCOHOLIC BEVERAGE CONTROL LAW

§102.  General prohibitions and restrictions

\* \* \* \* \* \* \* \* \* \* \* \*

2.  No person holding any license hereunder shall knowingly employ in connection with his business in any capacity whatsoever, any person, who has been convicted of a felony, or any of the following misdemeanors, or offenses, who has not subsequent to such conviction received an executive pardon therefor removing any civil disabilities incurred thereby or received the written approval of the state liquor authority permitting such employment, to wit:

(a)  Illegally using, carrying or possessing a pistol or other dangerous weapon;

(b)  Making or possessing burglar's instruments;

(c)  Buying or receiving stolen property;

(d)  Unlawful entry of a building;

(e)  Aiding escape from prison;

(f)  Unlawfully possessing or distributing habit forming narcotic drugs;

(g)  Violating subdivisions six, eight, ten or eleven of section seven hundred twenty-two of the penal law;

(h)  Vagrancy; or

(i)  Ownership, operation, possession, custody or control of a still subsequent to July first, nineteen hundred fifty-four. As amended L. 1954, c. 725 §1, eff. July 1, 1954.

EXHIBIT C

```
POLICE DEPARTMENT
CITY OF NEW YORK

- - - - - - - - - - - - - - - - - - - X

          In the Matter of

       BERIL W. RUBENSTEIN

For a Temporary Police Identification
Card and a Permanent Police Identifi-
cation Card.

- - - - - - - - - - - - - - - - - - - X


STATE OF NEW YORK )
COUNTY OF NEW YORK)  ss.  :
```

      BERIL W. RUBENSTEIN for his petition respectfully states:

    1. I am the Petitioner in the above entitled proceeding for a Temporary Identification Card and a Permanent Identification Card.

    2. I reside at No. 49 Grove Street, New York City with my wife Jean. We are expecting a child in February, 1958.

    3. I was arrested and subsequently convicted in December, 1951 and again on September 26, 1954 for the possession of marijuana. Since that time I have not been arrested. There has been no violation of law by me. I have had no further contact with marijuana nor have I freely or voluntarily associated with users of narcotics socially.

    4. I am a musician by profession and a pianist by training.

    5. When I was fourteen years of age, my father who was a Major in the Air Force died while serving our country in the Pacific theatre of operations. My mother subsequently never remarried. I was the eldest child in our family and the eldest son.

    A community which is undergoing the pressures

of war is never the ideal community for any adolescent to grow in. Added to this, however, was the fact that my father was killed in action as a noted hero and the public attention and pressure and the absence of parental control intensified the instability of what is always an unstable period of development.

I cannot state that I smoked reefers to escape financial difficulties. My family was well accepted in the community. I attended Syracuse University and was well regarded by instructors and fellow-students.

There was no justification for my involvement in narcotics. I have been advised by my physician that there was psychological pressures upon me which resulted in a temporary loss of social responsibility. That, however, is no longer the case. I am married. I have a good employment record. I enjoy my work. I am stable. I look forward to fatherhood within a few months. There is no need for me to indulge in narcotics nor will there ever be at any time hereafter.

This coming month, September, will mark the third anniversary of my arrest and I can truthfully state that this also marks a period of my life which is now conclusively over and in the past.

6. Employment opportunities are available to me in the City of New York on my obtaining a Temporary Identification Card.

7. As part of my petition, I submit additional affidavits and letters and exhibits as proof of the fact that I am now rehabilitated completely and am worthy of receiving the privilege of a Cabaret Identification Card.

As a happily married man I would like to work in an area which affords me the privileges of family life. New York City affords me that opportunity.

- 2 -

I, therefore, respectfully ask that there be
issued to me a Temporary Identification Card and a Permanent
Identification Card which will enable me to avail myself of
employment offered to me in the City of New York.

Dated: New York, N. Y.

August 28th, 1957.                    BERIL W. RUBENSTEIN
                                      P e t i t i o n e r .

POLICE DEPARTMENT
CITY OF NEW YORK

`- - - - - - - - - - - - - - - - - - - X`

     In the Matter of

    BERIL W. RUBENSTEIN

For a Temporary Police Identification
Card and a Permanent Police Identification Card.

`- - - - - - - - - - - - - - - - - - - X`

STATE OF NEW YORK )
COUNTY OF NEW YORK)  ss. :

        JEAN RUBENSTEIN, being duly sworn, deposes and
says:

        I am married to the Petitioner, Beril W. Rubenstein.

        I have lived with him since our marriage. He has
been consistently a devoted husband, conscientious in fulfilling
his responsibilities and completely stable and so very well adjusted that there is no indication that at one time in the past
there had been the instance of instability which resulted in his
narcotic arrest.

        I state this not out of wifely loyalty but because
this is a fact and this is one of the wonderful results of our
happy marriage. I am now pregnant, with child, and expect a baby
in February, 1958. We are looking forward to this event. It
means as much to us in our lives as it would in the lives of any
married couple. Of greater importance to us, however, is the
economic security which comes with parenthood and the need for
meeting medical and hospital bills and the added bills which will
come with the birth of the child.

EXHIBIT D-2

We live in New York City. We wish to live in
New York City. The stability of our household could only be main-
tained if my husband works in New York City.

His thorough rehabilitation, his complete abstin-
ence from narcotics, his assumption of the responsibilities of
good citizenship warrant his receiving permission to work in
New York City.

He has been accepted by his professional associates
as an accomplished pianist and musician and he feels, as others do,
that there will be professional development and growth in New York
City.

My husband has paid his debt to society for the
offenses committed. His present conduct has been exemplary and the
future holds forth greater responsibility and stability. The
future can be good for him, for myself and our child, if he is
made to feel that he is once more a member of society with a
right to work and the right to earn money to support his family
without feeling that he is perpetually a criminal, to be constantly
shunned and to be constantly marked-off as being different from
others.

I respectfully, therefore, ask for my husband,
myself and for my prospective family that he be given permission
to work in New York City.


Sworn to before me this
28th day of August, 1958.            _____JEAN RUBENSTEIN_____

CITY OF NEW YORK
POLICE DEPARTMENT

- - - - - - - - - - - - - - - - - - - X

In the Matter of the Petition of

     BERIL W. RUBENSTEIN,

                    Petitioner

For a Temporary Identification Card
and a Permanent Identification Card.

- - - - - - - - - - - - - - - - - - - X

STATE OF NEW YORK )
COUNTY OF NEW YORK) ss. :

        MAXWELL T. COHEN, being duly sworn, deposes and
says:

        I am an attorney duly admitted to practice in the
State of New York. I have been retained by BERIL W. RUBENSTEIN
with regard to this proceeding.

        I respectfully submit this affidavit with full
knowledge of the fact that there will be some degree of reliance
upon the representations made by me in this affidavit on behalf
of the petitioner. Accordingly, before accepting the petitioner
as a client, at his request, I made independent investigation
from very reliable sources as to the status of the petitioner, his
general reputation and character, his stability and as to the
existence of any rumors or facts pertaining to any alleged use of
narcotics or voluntary association with users of narcotics.

        I have, frankly, stated to the petitioner that I
reserve the right to withdraw as his attorney in the event that
his representations to me as to his rehabilitation were found to
be inaccurate.

EXHIBIT D-3

The fee charged the petitioner is not contingent
upon the success or failure of this proceeding.  No representation
has been made to the petitioner excepting the assurance that his
case would be given thorough and conscientious attention and preparation.

There are no disbursements with regard to this proceeding and the petitioner has been so advised.

A thorough investigation by me fails to reveal
the existence of any rumor which would point to or indicate that
the petitioner may be a user of narcotics.  On the contrary, he is
reputed to be a stable and conscientious individual, of good background, a very devoted husband and one well regarded in his profession.

Mrs. Rubenstein tells me that she and the petitioner
will become parents in February.  She has further informed me that
she knew of his background and difficulties and knew of his problems.  Certainly her association with the petitioner has been one
of the factors resulting in his stability and will certainly insure
a continuation of this stability.

When the petitioner was about fourteen years of
age, his father, a Major in the Air Corps, was killed in action.
The petitioner was the only son in the family and received an undue
amount of attention from his mother and the community.  The germ
of instability was planted at that time.

When he attended Syracuse University he freely
associated with a group of brilliant and neurotic students.  He
was easily susceptible to suggestions and attentions from them
and sought to compete with them with disasterous consequences.

In New York City he is far removed from Syracuse and the associations in Syracuse. He is happily married and can be gainfully employed. He is well regarded by other musicians and can obtain employment if he can obtain permission from the New York State Liquor Authority to obtain such employment.

Certainly whatever the personality problems may have been in the past which resulted in his anti-social behavior, they no longer exist and his reputation and character at the time of submitting this petition is exceedingly high. There are attached hereto letters and exhibits affirming this fact.

Because he has adjusted his life and rehabilitated himself thoroughly, the privilege of permission to work in New York City is respectfully sought in this proceeding.

A copy of this affidavit has been presented to the petitioner for his files.

Sworn to before me this
28th day of August, 1958.      _____ MAXWELL T. COHEN _____

EUGENE FREUNDLICH, M.D.
697 West End Avenue
New York 25, N. Y.

- - -

ACademy 2-3267

July 12, 1957

Police Department
City of New York

Gentlemen:

I examined Beril William Rubenstein today at my office, and I found him to be in excellent health. There is no evidence, on complete physical examination, of any use of narcotics. Skin shows no puncture marks. Pupils are normal. Reflexes are normal. Mental status is normal.

(Signed)      E. FREUNDLICH, M. D.

EXHIBIT D-4

New York, New York
August 1, 1957

New York City Police Department
To Whom it May Concern:

It gives me great pleasure to recommend
Billy Rubenstein. During the past seven years that I have known
him, I have always been impressed by his vigorous creative
ability, his sincerity and his broad perspective. He is rapidly
establishing for himself a place in the forefront of contemporary
American music. I feel certain that he will make a unique contribution to this field, since, as I have stated, he possesses all
of the qualifications necessary to speak profoundly in his creative
medium. In my opinion, he should be encouraged to practice his
art wherever and whenever possible.

As a performing artist, as well as a composer,
it is imperative that no areas of our culture be restricted to
him - - - on the contrary, every effort should be made to en-
courage him and to enable him to perform with other musicians,
most especially in the City of New York, a city which has always
been noted for its contribution to this phase of American culture.
I have been especially aware of his high regard for social responsibility during the last three years. This year particularly,
he has demonstrated a sincere awareness of the problems of
strengthening his moral fiber, thereby becoming a useful and
responsible citizen.

In conclusion, I sincerely feel that his present
high moral character and his unique creativity are a tribute to
the artistic expression of our country.

Sincerely,

(Signed)    ARIBERT P. MUNZER

ARIBERT P. MUNZER, Chairman
Department of Design
The Minneapolis School of Art
Minneapolis, Minnesota

APM:clv

EXHIBIT D-5

PEPSI-COLA COMPANY
3 West 57th Street
New York 19, N. Y.


Telephone Murray Hill 8-4500

July 12, 1957


Police Department
City of New York

To whom it may concern:

I have been asked by B. William Rubenstein to offer a written
statement with reference to his character, in connection with his
application for permission to perform in buildings which fall under
your jurisdiction.

I have known Bill Rubenstein since 1948, when we met at Syracuse
University, where we were classmates. I have been in continuing
contact with him since then, and am familiar with his professional
and personal career --- including his arrest for violation of the
narcotic laws.

Despite this unfortunate and youthful mistake, I consider him to
be a person of high moral character and integrity. I think his
record of successful and continuing employment during the past
several years is evidence of his strong desire to conduct his
life responsibly.

Early last year, I had the pleasure of being best man at his
marriage (performed by Dean Charles Noble of Syracuse University),
and have often been a guest in his home since then. I feel this
marriage offers further proof of his stability and good intentions.

With full appreciation of the aim and purpose of the laws to which
professional musicians are subject, I feel there is no risk whatsoever involved in allowing Bill Rubenstein to continue his
career unhampered by past misfortunes.

Respectfully submitted,

(Signed)     WILLIAM S. BROWN

William S. Brown
Sales Promotion Department


WSB:jt


EXHIBIT D-6

LETTER FROM RABBI BENJAMIN FRIEDMAN

August 12, 1957.

Police Department of the City of New York
New York, New York

Gentlemen:

I am writing in behalf of Mr. Beril W. Rubenstein who is a
pianist and anxious to play in New York City.

It is my sincere belief that Mr. Rubenstein will conduct himself
properly because he has gone through a trying period of rehabilitation. I have known Mr. Rubenstein almost from the time he was
born. His mother is a loyal member of my congregation. His
father was my dear personal friend who was killed in action in
the South Pacific. At that time he was a Major. When his father
died, Mr. Rubenstein lost not only a wonderful father, but a
great guiding influence. It is true that as a young man he
became involved in trouble. I helped him during this period and
feel that my efforts have been justified. During his last visit
to Syracuse I spoke to him and am convinced that he will be no
longer a problem to anyone. He deserves our faith in the power
of rehabilitation.

It is my earnest hope that you will view with favor his desire
to pursue his professional career in New York.

                                   Sincerely yours,

                   (signed)    BENJAMIN FRIEDMAN

                               Benjamin Friedman

BF:st

July 22, 1957

Police Department
New York City
New York

Dear Sir:

      As the Clergyman who officiated at
Mr. Beril W. Rubenstein's marriage, and who counselled both
Mr. and Mrs. Rubenstein, I am happy to report that, in my judgment, Mr. Rubenstein has been completely rehabilitated. From my
observations, Mr. Rubenstein is entirely free of the habits and
influences which induced his former delinquency.

                         Respectfully yours,

               (Signed)    CHARLES C. NOBLE
                       CHARLES C. NOBLE

CCN:cdh

EXHIBIT D-8

ONONDAGA COUNTY COURT

LEO W. BREED
ONONDAGA COUNTY JUDGE

**PROBATION DEPARTMENT**
~~441 MONTGOMERY~~ STREET
SYRACUSE 2, N. Y.

GEORGE H. CAIN
CHIEF PROBATION OFFICER

PHONE 2-1121

August 20, 1957

Chief of Police
Police Department
New York City

Dear Sir:                    Re: Petition for License

                             Beril W. Rubenstein

I am informed by this applicant that he requires a permit
to continue employment as a pianist in New York City.

Subject was arrested at Syracuse September 26th, 1954 on
suspicion that his car contained marijuana cigarets. He
was paroled and continued travelling with his band. On
November 29th, 1955 subject appeared in Court of Special
Sessions at Syracuse and pleaded guilty to unlawful
possession of narcotics. Sentence of one year to Onondaga
County Penitentiary was suspended and probation ordered
for a term of one year.

My experience with this young man convinced me he was an
honest, upright citizen diligently following his chosen
profession as a pianist. He reported regularly at our
office as required; reported regularly by mail when on the
road; kept me informed of his whereabouts. I met his mother
and know that he came of a good family living in an exclusive
residential part of Syracuse.

Eventually subject brought a young lady to meet me as his
wife. She was formerly a social worker in the State of
Connecticut. Our relations were always agreeable and I
have only high regard for Beril Rubenstein and was glad
to approve his honorable discharge from probation at the
conclusion of one year.

I heartily recommend your favorable consideration of his
application for a license to continue employment as a
pianist.

                             Very truly yours,


                             Chief Probation Officer
                             Onondaga County Courts

GHG
cc           EXHIBIT D-9

COURT OF SPECIAL SESSIONS
OF THE CITY OF SYRACUSE,
COUNTY OF ONONDAGA, NEW YORK

The People of the State of New York

against

Beril Rubenstein ·

SS.

Janruary 15th　，19 52

The above named ................ Beril Rubenstein ................ having been brought before

Hon. William H. Bamerick, Justice of Special Sessions of the City of Syracuse, in the County of Onondaga, New

York, charged with ..... Violation of Section 422 of the Public Health Law
and thereby violating Section 1751-A of the Penal Law of the State
of New York, in that said defendant did then and there wilfully and
unlawfully have in his possession a Narcotic Drug, to-wit: A
quantity of Canabis Sativa in the city of Syracuse, N.Y.

And the above named ......... Beril Rubenstein ......... having been thereupon duly convicted,

upon a plea of guilty. It is adjudged that　he pay a fine of ..... Five Hundred ($500.00) ..... dollars
**and be** ..................................... Six (6) Months
imprisoned in the Onondaga County Penitentiary xxxxxxxxxxxxxxxxxxxxxxxxXXXXXXXXXXXXxxxx.

Dated at the City of Syracuse, New York, the 15 day of ..... January ..... , 19 52

/s/ WILLIAM H. BAMERICK

Justice of Special Sessions.
Clerk of the Court of Special Sessions
City of Syracuse, New York.

STATE OF NEW YORK
COUNTY OF ONONDAGA 〉·····ss
CITY OF S RACUSE

　　　I hereby certify that I have compared the foregoing with the
original record of the Court of Special Sessions, and that the same
is a correct copy thereof and transcript therefrom and of the whole
thereof.

Witness my hand this 15th day of July 1957　*Herbert A. Johnson*

Herbert A. Johnson
Deputy Clerk
Court Special Sessions
City of Syracuse, N.Y.

EXHIBIT D-10

COURT OF SPECIAL SESSIONS
OF THE CITY OF SYRACUSE,
COUNTY OF ONONDAGA, NEW YORK

The People of the State of New York
against
**Beril Wm. Rubenstein**

November 29th, 19 55

The above named **Beril Wm. Rubenstein** having been brought before

Hon. Leo Dorsey, Justice of Special Sessions of the City of Syracuse, in the County of Onondaga, New York,

charged with Violation of Section 3305 Article 33 of the Public Health law, thereby violating Section 1751-a of the Penal Law of the State of New York, in that he did then and there wilfully and unlawfully have in his possession a Narcotic Drug to-wit: 2 Marihuana Cigarettes and 1 Vial containg Marihuana, at E. Fayette & S. Salina St. in the City of Syracuse, N.Y.

And the above named **Beril Wm. Rubenstein** having been thereupon duly convicted,

upon a plea of guilty. It is adjudged that ~~he be imprisoned~~ Imprisonment in the Onondaga County Penitentiary for one (1) year be and is hereby suspended, and said defendant placed on probation for one (1) Year, to Onondaga County Probation Dept.

Dated at the City of Syracuse, New York, the 29 day of November, 19 55

/s/ P. LEO DORSEY
Justice of Special Sessions.
~~Clerk of the Court of Special Sessions.~~
City of Syracuse, New York.

N-31
DUPLICATE

State of New York )
County of Onondaga )....ss
City of Syracuse, N)

I hereby certify that I have compared the foregoing with the original record of the Court of Special Sessions, and that the same is a correct copy thereof and transcript therefrom and of the whole thereof.

Witness my hand this 15th day of July 1957

Herbert A. Johnson
Deputy Clerk
Court Special Sessions
City Syracuse, New York

EXHIBIT D-11

POLICE DEPARTMENT
City of New York
New York 13, N.Y.

DIVISION OF LICENSES
Cabaret & Dance Hall Bureau
156 Greenwich Street
New York 6, New York

November 18, 1957.

Mr. Beril Rubenstein,
49 Grove Street,
New York City, N.Y.

Dear Sir:

       Reference is made to the hearing that was held
on October 16, 1957 at this bureau in the matter of your application for a Cabaret Employee's Identification Card.

       Please be advised that the decision of this
hearing is the disapproval of the application.

                   Very truly yours,

       (Signed)     CHARLES CROWLEY

                Charles Crowley
                Lieutenant

CC/ac

EXHIBIT **F**

Law Offices

MAXWELL T. COHEN
505 Fifth Avenue
New York 17, N.Y.

MUrray Hill 2-1800                                    November 21st, 1957.

The Deputy Commissioner,
Bureau of Licensing,
The Police Department,
156 Greenwich Street,
New York City.

Re: BERYL W. RUBENSTEIN,
Applicant for ID Card.

Dear Sir:

Pursuant to our phone conversation this morning,
may I respectfully request a re-review of the Applicant's petition, the exhibits admitted at the Hearing which included the
SLA Employment permit, and the Memorandum submitted at the
Hearing.

Although I did not receive notification of the
Department's decision, my client did receive notification of
denial and so informed me.

I would appreciate a reply to this letter and its
request for re-review.

Yours truly,

(Signed)   MAXWELL T. COHEN

MAXWELL T. COHEN

EXHIBIT G

POLICE DEPARTMENT
CITY OF NEW YORK
NEW YORK 13, N.Y.


December 23, 1957


Maxwell T. Cohen
Attorney At Law
505 Fifth Avenue
New York 17, N. Y.

RE: Beril W. Rubenstein

Dear Sir:

      Replying to your letter of December 19th
relative to the application of the above named person for a
cabaret employee identification card, I wish to advise that
after a careful examination of the records I find no reason
for any modification of the original decision in the case.


                  Sincerely yours,

      (Signed)      JAMES McELROY

                  James McElroy
                  Deputy Commissioner
                  in Charge of Licenses


W.


EXHIBIT H

**POLICE DEPARTMENT**
CITY OF NEW YORK
NEW YORK 13, N. Y.

DIVISION OF LICENSES
156 Greenwich Street
New York 6, New York

August 11, 1958

Maxwell T. Cohen, Esq.
505 Fifth Avenue
New York, New York

Re: Beril Rubenstein

Dear Sir:

I have carefully studied your letter of petition
of July 8th, and previous correspondence in connection
with application of above-named person for a Cabaret
Employee's Identification Card, together with the
criminal record of the applicant and regret to advise
you that I can find no reason to change the previous
decision in this case.

Sincerely yours,

James McElroy
Deputy Commissioner.

JME:vw

EXHIBIT "I".

POLICE DEPARTMENT
CITY OF NEW YORK
NEW YORK 13, N. Y.

DIVISION OF LICENSES
156 Greenwich Street
New York 6, New York

August 15, 1958

Mr. Maxwell T. Cohen
505 Fifth Avenue
New York, New York

Re: Beril Rubenstein

Dear Sir:

Your telegram of August 12th, addressed
to the Police Commissioner, has been directed to
the attention of the undersigned.

If there is any new developments concerning
your client, you will be given an opportunity to
present them at this office on Friday, August 22nd,
at 10:00 a.m. when Mr. Rubenstein should be present.

Sincerely yours,

Louis McElroy
Deputy Commissioner.

JME:vw

EXHIBIT "J".

**POLICE DEPARTMENT**
CITY OF NEW YORK
NEW YORK 13, N. Y.

DIVISION OF LICENSES
156 Greenwich Street
New York 6, New York

September 9, 1958

Maxwell T. Cohen, Esq.
505 Fifth Avenue
New York, New York

Re: Beril Rubenstein

Dear Sir:

I have carefully examined the petition briefs
and representations made by you and your client at
the latest re-hearing held at this office on
August 25, 1958 and have carefully re-examined the
record of your client and am forced to the conclusion
that no further change should be made in the previous
decision reached in this matter.

Sincerely yours,

James McElroy
Deputy Commissioner.

JME:vw

EXHIBIT "K".

EXHIBIT "L".

RESTRICTED TO EMPLOYMENT AT:

CABARET
DANCE HALL _Smalls Paradise_

ADDRESS _7th Ave. + 135th St. N.Y._

JUN 1 2 1958

POLICE DEPARTMENT
DIVISION OF LICENSES
156 GREENWICH STREET
NEW YORK 6, N.Y.

L. D. 76 (Rev. 3-57)

G _1801_
(PERMIT NUMBER)

# ABOUT THE AUTHOR

MAXWELL T. COHEN was awarded a plaque at the Newport Jazz Festival by the New York Jazz Museum for defending the civil rights of musicians and other performing artists. He was also cited and received an Award of Appreciation from the Society of Black Composers. Cohen was the attorney for Duke Ellington, Dizzy Gillespie, and other jazz artists. Cohen's previous book, *Race and Religion in Adoption Proceedings,* was instrumental in the elimination of restrictive religious and racial laws in adoption and other similar proceedings. Professor Cohen was awarded an Honorary Degree of Doctor of Laws and Letters by the State University of New York and an international Commendation for his work in international human rights by The Center for Research in Religious and Human Rights in Closed Societies. Maxwell T. Cohen taught Law and Social Problems and Social Issues at the State University of New York and the City University of New York. He is presently Professor of Constitutional Law and Sociology at Northampton Community College in Pennsylvania.